The Decline of the
Welfare State

The Decline of the Welfare State

Demography and Globalization

Assaf Razin and
Efraim Sadka
in cooperation with
Chang Woon Nam

CESifo Book Series

The MIT Press
Cambridge, Massachusetts
London, England

This book was set in Palatino on 3B2 by Asco Typesetters, Hong Kong, and was printed and bound in the United States of America.

Library of Congress Cataloging-in-Publication Data

Razin, Assaf.
  The decline of the welfare state : demography and globalization / Assaf Razin and Efraim Sadka ; in cooperation with Chang Woon Nam.
    p.   cm. — (CESifo book series)
  Includes bibliographical references and index.
  ISBN 0-262-18244-0 (hc. : alk. paper)
  1. Welfare state. 2. Aging. 3. Emigration and immigration. 4. Globalization.
I. Sadka, Efraim. II. Nam, Ch. W. III. Title. IV. Series.
JC479.R39   2005
330.12′6—dc22   2004055166

10 9 8 7 6 5 4 3 2 1

Contents

Preface

The modern welfare state redistributes income from the working young to the retired old and from the rich to the poor. Aging—a common contemporary phenomenon in the industrial countries—has far-reaching implications for the survival of the welfare state. Similarly, though to a lesser degree, low-skill migration attracted to the welfare state may put additional strains on it. Finally, globalization—another widespread recent phenomenon—generates international tax competition, and the consequent erosion in the tax base, especially on capital income, is another blow to the public finance of the welfare state.

This book provides an integrated political-economy framework for analyzing the welfare state. The unified framework addresses a set of important and interrelated topics—how aging, migration, and globalization affect the size and sources of financing of the modern welfare state. The book demonstrates how demography and globalization are teaming up to downscale the size of the welfare state and change its various tax pillars.

In writing this book, we greatly benefited from previous collaborations with Phillip Swagel, including "Tax Burden and Migration: A Political-Economy Theory and Evidence," *Journal of Public Economics* 85(2) (August 2002): 167–190; "The Aging Population and the Size of the Welfare State," *Journal of Political Economy* 110(4) (August 2002): 900–918; "The Wage Gap and Social Security: Theory and Evidence," *American Economic Review: Papers and Proceedings* 92(2) (May 2002): 390–395; and "Capital Income Taxation: Aging and the Mixed Attitude of the Old," *The Review of World Economics*, 140 (3), (September 2004).

We also draw on our previous works, "Interactions between International Migration and the Welfare State," in Slobodan Djajic, ed., *International Migration: Trends, Policy and Economic Impact* (New York: Routledge, 2001), and "The Stability and Growth Pact as an Impediment to Privatizing Social Security," Working Paper 9278, National Bureau of Economic Research, Cambridge, MA (October 2002).

We wish to thank Chang Woon Nam for collaborating with us on issues of capital taxation in Europe. Part of the work on the book was done when we visited the Economic Policy Research Unit (EPRU) at the University of Copenhagen in February 2003. We wish to thank EPRU and its director, Peter Birch Sorensen, for their hospitality. We thank also the European research grant, RTN Contract No. HPRN-CT-1999-0067, for research on "The Analysis of International Capital Markets." We wish also to thank the Center for Economic Studies and the Ifo Institute for Economic Research (CESifo) in Munich for providing financial support. Stella Padeh patiently and competently typed the manuscript.

Finally, Hans-Werner Sinn, the director of CESifo, initiated the idea to write this book and provided continuous encouragement throughout the time we spent at CESifo. We thank him wholeheartedly.

October 2003
Assaf Razin
Efraim Sadka
Tel Aviv, Israel

The Decline of the
Welfare State

1   Overview

In the coming decades, the population of the industrialized world is forecast to age dramatically. In the European Union (EU), before the 2004 enlargement, old-age dependency—defined as the ratio of people age sixty and older to people age 15 through 59—is projected to rise from 35 percent in 2000 to 66 percent in 2050. Within the European Union, aging is expected to be most pronounced in Germany, Italy, and Spain, where this ratio is forecast to rise to 71, 76, and 81 percent, respectively, by 2050. Aging trends are almost as severe in Japan, where old-age dependency is forecast to rise from 36 to 70 percent over the same period. In comparison, projected population trends in the United States look almost benign. The U.S. Census Bureau currently forecasts that the U.S. old-age dependency ratio will reach 47 percent in 2050, up from 27 percent in 2000.[1]

The aging of the population has far-reaching implications for national pension systems.[2] In continental Europe, most state pension systems are unfunded (pay-as-you-go systems), and the benefits are generous. Dramatic increases in old-age dependency will necessitate a sharp rise in taxes if benefits are maintained largely intact. The Organization for Economic Cooperation and Development (OECD) predicts that France, for example, will have to spend 33 percent more, as a share of gross domestic product (GDP), than it does now. The income and payroll taxes that support Europe's large welfare states drive a deep wedge between a worker's take-home wage and the much higher costs of employing her.

Similarly, in many other countries, the simulated tax-contribution rates that would balance the old-age social security systems are significantly higher than the statutory rates. For example, Agar Brugiavini (1999) reports that this simulated rate reached 44 percent for Italy in 1991. Another dimension of the financial burden is the public debt (*The Economist*, 2002, p. 22): "On some estimates, by 2050, government debt could be equivalent to almost 100 percent of national income in America, 150 percent in the EU as a whole, and over 250 percent in Germany and France." To put these staggering figures in perspective, recall that the European Union's 1997 Stability and Growth Pact puts a 60 percent target ceiling on public debt as a percentage of national income![3]

A comprehensive study conducted recently by Jagadeesh Gokhale and Kent Smetters (2003) takes into account all current liabilities and projected future expenditures of the U.S. government and compares them with all the revenues that the government can expect to collect in the future. The difference (in present value) is a staggering deficit of $44 trillion—almost quadruple the U.S. gross national product (GNP).[4] Major contributing factors to this deficit are old-age social security and medical care.

Similarly, widespread low-skill migration also strains the public finances of the welfare state. A recent estimate of the likely inflow of immigrants from the 2004 entrants to the EU (excluding Malta and Cyprus), Bulgaria and Romania, put the figure for gross inflows at 340,000 immigrants per year (see Hille and Straubhaar [2001]). Being relatively low earners, migrants are typically net beneficiaries of the welfare state—that is, they are expected to receive benefits in excess of the taxes (contributions) they pay. For instance, a recent study initiated by the U.S. National Research Council estimates that the overall net fiscal burden of migrants (age twenty through forty years, with less than high school education on arrival) is about $60,000 to $150,000 over their lifetimes (see Smith and Edmonston, 1997).

As the share of elderly people in the population rises when the population ages, their political clout would be expected to strengthen the pro-welfare-state coalition. Similarly, this coalition would be expected to gain more political power as more low-skill migrants are naturalized. Thus, aging and migration seem to tilt the political power balance in the direction of boosting the welfare state, imposing a growing burden on the existing workforce. However, the theme that is put forth in this book is quite the opposite: aging and low-skill migration generate indirectly political processes that trim rather than boost the size of the welfare state. We reach this somewhat surprising conclusion by carefully working through a conventional model of a political-economy determination of the welfare state. We also provide some supportive empirical evidence from the European Union and the United States for this general theme.

But what if the welfare state tries to rely on capital taxes to finance the social benefits that it provides? Recall that the old derive most of their income from capital because they retired from work. At first, it may seem that as the share of the old in an aging population rises, an attempt to rely on capital taxes would face stiffer political resistance. However, after carefully scrutinizing this hypothesis, we come to an unexpected conclusion: aging plausibly tilts the political-power balance in favor of a larger capital-financed welfare state. We provide supportive empirical evidence from the European Union for this conclusion.

Is this conclusion relevant? Not entirely. After all, aging is not the only process witnessed nowadays. Globalization across various economies is another universal phenomenon that must be reckoned with.[5] Can high capital taxes survive international tax competition brought about by such globalization? Evidently, in the absence of worldwide tax coordination and enforcement, the answer is no[6] (*The Economist*, 1997, pp. 17–18):

Globalization is a tax problem for three reasons. First, firms have more freedom over where to locate.... This will make it harder for a country to tax [a business] much more heavily than its competitors.... Second, globalization makes it hard to decide where a company should pay tax, regardless of where it is based.... This gives them [the companies] plenty of scope to reduce tax bills by shifting operations around or by crafting transfer-pricing.... [Third], globalization ... nibbles away at the edges of taxes on individuals. It is harder to tax personal income because skilled professional workers are more mobile than they were two decades ago.

The 2004 enlargement of the EU gives a stark example for the underlying downward pressure of tax competition. The new entrants have significantly lower corporate tax rates (zero in Estonia, for instance) than the original EU-15 countries (40% in Germany). It seems inevitable that the high-tax countries will have to succumb to the forces of tax competition and sharply cut their corporate tax rates.

Thus, we apply our political-economy model again to assess the forces of globalization. The combined forces of aging, low-skill migration, and globalization seem to be too strong for the welfare state to survive in its present size.

Indeed, most of the large industrialized economies have embarked in recent years on a track of trimming the generosity of their pension and other welfare-state programs. The general rules are quite straightforward: raise the retirement age, and curtail benefits. Following the report of the bipartisan Greenspan Committee (January 1983), the United States has gradually raised the retirement age so that it will reach sixty-seven in the year 2027.[7] Similarly but much later, France decided in July 2003 to require public-sector workers (about one-fourth of the French workforce) to contribute to the state pension system for forty years instead of 37.5 years. Germany, which has already raised its retirement age from sixty-three to sixty-five, recently decided to raise it further to sixty-seven between 2011 and 2035. With respect to curtailing benefits, this is usually accomplished by abandoning wage indexation in favor of price indexation (or by subjecting benefits to income taxation). Naturally, wages typically rise faster than prices (due mostly to productivity increases) so that each new cohort of retirees gets a starting benefit level with greater purchasing power than the previous cohort's starting benefit level. Thus, price indexation is less generous than wage indexation to pensioners (see Cogan and Mitchell, 2003, for the United States and Thode, 2003, for Europe). With respect to tax increases, currently in the United States only the first $87,900 of annual wages is subject to the social security tax. The social security tax, as it stands now, is regressive. At the center of the public debate is correcting this aspect as a way to strengthen the social security trust fund, to pay benefits once the baby boomers retire. A favored solution among conservatives is to allow individuals to invest part or all of the tax they would have to pay in private investment accounts instead.

As we examine the decline of the welfare state from a political-economy perspective, we uncover in this book how the processes of aging and globalization (through migration, capital mobility, and international tax competition) team up to change the political-power balance and generate public support for reforming the welfare state.

I   Political Economics

2

Aging, Migration, and the Widening Wage Gap

2.1 Introduction

The modern welfare state typically redistributes income from the rich to the poor and from the young to the old, either by cash or by in-kind transfers. With the aging of the population, the proportion of voters receiving social security has increased, and these pensions are by far the largest component of transfers in all industrial economies. Jim Oeppen and James W. Vaupel (2002) have noticed that life expectancy in the countries where people already live longest has risen by a constant two-and-a-half years per decade since 1840.

Indeed, as mentioned in the previous chapter, the median age in Europe is forecasted to rise from 37.7 now to 52.7 in 2050 (*The Economist*, 2002, p. 22). Similarly, the ratio of the elderly (age sixty years and over) to the working-age population (age fifteen through fifty-nine years) in western Europe is expected to double from 20 percent in the year 2000 to 40 percent in the year 2050 (*The Economist*, 2002, p. 22). These demographic trends are driven by declining fertility rates (*The Economist*, 2002, p. 11):[1]

At present, West European countries are following what seems to be a normal demographic path: As they became richer after the 1950s, so their fertility rates fell sharply. The average number of children borne by each woman during her lifetime fell from well above the "replacement rate" of 2.1—the rate at which the population remains stable—to less than 1.4 now.

The income-redistribution feature of the welfare state makes it an attractive destination, particularly for low-skill immigrants. For example, a study by George Borjas (1994) indicates that foreign-born households in the United States accounted for 10 percent of households receiving public assistance in 1990 and for 13 percent of total cash assistance distributed, even though they constituted only 8 percent of all households in the United States.

The growth of the welfare state coincided with increased returns to education and thus with broader wage differentials between workers with relatively high levels of skills or education and those without. These differentials were further boosted by skill-biased technical changes and globalization.

This chapter provides a political-economy framework that conceptually connects these phenomena. We show how in a democratic framework the aging of the population, the widening of the wage gap, and low-skill migration all affect the political-economy determination of the tax rates and the generosity of transfers.

We discovered that an aging population and low-skill migration have similar effects on the political-economy equilibrium tax rates and transfers. On the one hand, an aging population or a higher share of low-skill migrants means a larger protax coalition because the retired and low-skill migrants are net beneficiaries of transfers from those who are employed. On the other hand, an aging population or a higher share of low-skill migrants puts a higher tax burden on the median voter because it becomes necessary to finance transfers to a larger share of the population. People for whom the costs of higher taxes outweigh the benefits shift to the antitax coalition. Hence, it may well be that the second factor dominates and that the political-economy equilibrium tax rate declines when the dependency ratio or the share of low-skill migrants rises.

The effect of a widening wage gap on the political-economy equilibrium tax and benefit depends on whether the median voter is skilled or not: when she is skilled, the tax rate and the benefit decline; when she is not skilled, the opposite is true. These hypotheses are supported by our empirical analysis. Using panel data on the United States and ten European countries in the 1970s, 1980s, and 1990s, we provide supportive empirical evidence.

2.2   Tax-Transfer Policy in a Political-Economy Equilibrium

Consider a standard overlapping-generations model in which each generation lives two periods—a working period and a retirement period. Following Gilles Saint-Paul (1994) and Assaf Razin and Efraim Sadka (1995b), we assume a stylized economy in which there are two types of workers: skilled workers have high productivity and provide one efficiency unit of labor per each unit of labor time, and unskilled workers have low productivity and provide only $q < 1$ efficiency units of labor per each unit of labor time. Workers have one unit of labor time during their first period of life but are born without skills and thus with low productivity. Each worker chooses whether to acquire an education and become a skilled worker or to remain unskilled. After the working period, individuals retire, with their consumption funded by savings from their earnings and a government transfer (discussed below).

There is a continuum of individuals that is characterized by an innate ability parameter e, which is the time needed to acquire an education. By investing e units of labor time in education, a worker becomes skilled, after which the remaining $1 - e$ units of labor time provide an equal amount of effective labor. Less capable individuals require more time to become skilled and thus find education more costly in terms of lost income (education is a full-time activity). We assume a positive pecuniary cost of acquiring skills γ, which is not tax-deductible.[2] The cumulative distribution function of innate ability is denoted by $G(e)$, with the support being the interval $[0, 1]$. The density function is denoted by $g = G'$.

Suppose that the government levies a flat tax on labor income to finance a flat grant b. The literature (e.g., Mirrlees, 1971) suggests that the best egalitarian income tax can be approximated by a linear tax that consists of a flat rate τ and a lump-sum cash grant b. The tax rate and generosity of the grant are linked through the government's budget constraint. In a multiperiod setting, this simple specification captures the spirit of a pay-as-you-go, tax-benefit (transfer) system. The features of the transfer can include a uniform per-capita grant (either in cash or in kind, such as national health care), as well as age-related benefits such as old-age social security and medial care or free public education.[3] If an e individual (namely, an individual with an education-cost parameter e) decides to become skilled, then her after-tax income is $(1 - \tau)w(1 - e) + b - \gamma$, where w is the wage rate per efficiency unit of labor. If she remains unskilled, her after-tax income is $(1 - \tau)qw + b$. Note that acquiring a skill is more attractive for individuals who have low costs of education than for individuals who have high costs.

Thus, there exists a cutoff level e^* such that those with education-cost parameter below e^* invest in education and become skilled, whereas everyone else remains unskilled. The cutoff level is the cost-of-education parameter of an individual who is indifferent between becoming skilled or not:

$$(1 - \tau)w(1 - e^*) + b - \gamma = (1 - \tau)qw + b.$$

Rearranging terms gives the cutoff level for the education decision:

$$e^* = 1 - q - \frac{\gamma}{(1 - \tau)w}. \tag{2.1}$$

Note that the higher the tax rate is, the lower e^* is. That is, the fraction of skilled workers in the labor force falls with the tax rate.

To obtain analytical results, we must use a specification in which factor prices are not variable.[4] Thus, for analytical tractability, we assume that the production function is effectively linear in labor L and capital K:

$$Y = wL + (1 + r)K, \tag{2.2}$$

where Y is gross output. The wage rate w and the gross rental price of capital $1 + r$ are determined by the marginal productivity conditions for factor prices ($w = \partial Y / \partial L$ and $1 + r = \partial Y / \partial K$) and are already substituted into the production function. The linearity of the production function can arise as an equilibrium outcome through either international capital mobility or factor price equalization arising from goods' trade. For simplicity, the two types of labor are assumed to be perfect substitutes in production in terms of efficiency units of labor input, and capital is assumed to depreciate fully at the end of the production process.

We assume that the population grows at a rate of n. Because individuals work only in the first period, the ratio of retirees to workers is $1/(1 + n)$, and the (old-young) dependency ratio— retired as a share of the total population—equals $1/(2 + n)$. Note also that $(1 - q)w$ is a measure of the wage gap. Our analysis focuses on the effects of the dependency ratio and the wage gap on the political-economy equilibrium.

Each individual's labor supply is assumed to be fixed, so that the income tax does not distort individual labor-supply decisions at the margin. The total labor supply does, however, depend on the income-tax rate, as this affects the cutoff cost-of-education parameter e^* and thus the mix of skilled and unskilled in the economy. This can be seen from equation (2.1), which implies that e^* is declining in τ, so that the tax transfer is distortive.[5] Note also that an increase in τ reduces the share of the skilled individuals in the labor force. This, in turn, reduces the effective labor supply and output. In period t, the total labor supply is given by

$$L_t = \left\{ \int_0^{e_t^*} (1 - e)\, dG + q[1 - G(e_t^*)] \right\} N_0 (1 + n)^t$$

$$= \ell(e_t^*) N_0 (1 + n)^t, \tag{2.3}$$

where $N_0(1 + n)^t$ is the size of the working-age population in period t (with N_0 the number of young individuals n period 0), and

$l(e_t^*) = \int_0^{e_t^*} (1 - e)\,dG + q[1 - G(e_t^*)]$ is the average (per-worker) labor supply in period t. This specification implies that for each e and t, the number of individuals in period t who have a cost-of-education parameter less than or equal to e is $(1 + n)^t$ times the number of such individuals in period 0.

The government's budget is balanced period by period. Since the income tax is levied on labor income, the wage bill wL_t constitutes the tax base. The cash grant is paid to both workers and retirees, so that the government budget constraint implies

$$b_t N_0[(1 + n)^{t-1} + (1 + n)^t] = \tau_t w L_t$$

$$= \tau_t w l(e_t^*) N_0 (1 + n)^t.$$

Therefore, the lump-sum grant equals

$$b_t = \tau_t w l(e_t^*)(1 + n)/(2 + n). \tag{2.4}$$

The assumption that the benefit is paid to both young and old is essential for obtaining an equilibrium with positive tax and benefit. For if the benefit is paid only to the old, then in the political-economy equilibrium the young (who outnumber the old in a growing economy) will drive the tax and the transfer down to zero. An alternative specification is to assume that the benefit is paid only to the old but that a credible implicit social contract leads the current young to expect to receive a retirement benefit equaling the one that they are presently voting on to pay the current old. We may thus conjecture that "bundling" together benefits to young and old is essential for establishing an incentive-compatible social contract or norm in which the current young engage in redistribution to the old with the anticipation that the future young will honor the "contract." In reality, some bundling together of benefits to the young and old indeed occurs. For example, the payroll social security tax serves to finance both old-age transfers and unemployment benefits (and national health care in many countries).

For any tax rate τ, dependency ratio n, and wage gap q, equations (2.1) and (2.4) determine $e_t^* = e^*(\tau_t, q)$ and $b_t = b(\tau_t, n, q)$ as functions of τ_t, n, and q. The population growth rate n and the productivity parameter q are exogenous, but we explore the effect of changes in these parameters on the political-economy equilibrium.

Denote by $W(e, \tau_t, \tau_{t+1}, n, q)$ the after-tax lifetime income of an individual born at period t with education-cost parameter e. This is a strictly decreasing function of e for the skilled worker and is constant for the unskilled worker. (Note that for all people who remain unskilled, the education-cost parameter is irrelevant and they all have the same after-tax lifetime income.) This net after-tax lifetime income is given by

$$
W(e, \tau_t, \tau_{t+1}, n, q) = \begin{cases} (1 - \tau)w(1 - e) - \gamma + b(\tau_t, n, q) + \dfrac{b(\tau_{t+1}, n, q)}{(1 + r)} \\[2mm] \quad \text{for } e \leqq e^*(\tau_t, q) \\[4mm] (1 - \tau)wq + b(\tau_t, n, q) + \dfrac{b(\tau_{t+1}, n, q)}{(1 + r)} \\[2mm] \quad \text{for } e \geqq e^*(\tau_t, q). \end{cases}
$$

$$(2.5)$$

(See figure 2.1.)

A young individual born in period t chooses her first- and second-period consumption $u(c_{1t}, c_{2t})$, subject to the lifetime budget constraint $c_{1t} + c_{2t}/(1 + r) = W(e, \tau_t, \tau_{t+1}, n, q)$.

Second-period consumption of a retiree born in period $t - 1$ (that is, consumption of a retiree in period t) is given by

$$c_{2,t-1}(e, n, q) = S_{t-1}(e, n, q)(1 + r) + b(\tau_t, n, q), \tag{2.6}$$

where $S_{t-1}(e, n, q)$ denotes this individual's savings in period $t - 1$.

Because the government's budget constraint is balanced period by period, it follows that the transfer in period $t + 1$, $b(\tau_{t+1}, n, q)$ is independent of the tax rate τ_t in period t. In voting on the tax rate τ_t, individuals living in period t therefore take $b(\tau_{t+1}, n, q)$ as exogenous because there is no serial correlation between $b(\tau_t, n, q)$ and $b(\tau_{t+1}, n, q)$. The political-economy equilibrium for the tax rate τ_t is then determined by majority voting of individuals alive in period t, without being affected by preceding or future generations.

We therefore calculate the effect of taxes on the income of any young individual to find how she will vote on a proposed change in the tax rate. Differentiating $W(e, \tau_t, \tau_{t+1}, n, q)$ with respect to e and τ_t, we find that

$$\frac{\partial^2 W(e, \tau_t, \tau_{t+1}, n, q)}{\partial e \partial \tau_t} = \begin{cases} w & \text{for } 0 \le e < e^*(\tau_t, q) \\ 0 & \text{for } e^*(\tau_t, q) < e < 1. \end{cases}$$

Therefore, if $\partial W / \partial \tau_t > 0$ for some e_o, then $\partial W / \partial \tau_t > 0$ for all $e > e_o$. And similarly, if $\partial W / \partial \tau_t < 0$ for some e_o, then $\partial W / \partial \tau_t < 0$ for all $e < e_o$. This implies that if an increase in the income-tax rate benefits a particular young (working) individual (because the resulting higher transfer more than offsets the tax hike), then all young individuals who are less able (that is, those who have a higher education-cost parameter e) must also gain from this tax increase. Similarly, if an income-tax increase hurts a certain young individual (because the increased transfer does not fully compensate for the tax hike), then it must also hurt all young individuals who are more able (who have a lower education-cost parameter).

As long as raising the tax rate in period t (that is, τ_t) generates more revenues and, consequently, a higher grant in that period $b(\tau_t, n)$, it follows from equation (2.6) that the old (retirees) in period t always opt for a higher tax rate in that period. As long as $n > 0$, it follows that there are always more young (working) people than old (retired) people. These considerations imply that the median voter—the pivot (decisive voter) in determining the outcome of majority voting—is a young (working) individual. That is, the political-economy-equilibrium tax rate maximizes the after-tax lifetime income of the median voter who is a young (working) individual.[6]

Denote the education-cost parameter of this median voter by e_M. There are $N_0(1 + n)^t G(e_M)$ young individuals with education-cost parameter $e \le e_M$ (more able than the median voter) and $N_0(1 + n)^t [1 - G(e_M)]$ young individuals with an education-cost parameter $e \ge e_M$ (less able than the median). There are also $N_0(1 + n)^{t-1}$ retired individuals in period t who always join the protax coalition. Hence, e_M is defined implicitly by

$$N_0(1 + n)^t G(e_M) = N_0[1 + n]^t[1 - G(e_M)] + N_0(1 + n)^{t-1}.$$

Dividing this equation by $N_0(1 + n)^{t-1}$ and rearranging terms yields the education-cost parameter for the median voter:

$$e_M(n) = G^{-1}\left[\frac{2 + n}{2(1 + n)}\right]. \tag{2.7}$$

As noted, the political-equilibrium tax rate τ in period t—denoted by $\tau_o(n, q)$—maximizes the after-tax lifetime income of the median voter:

$$\tau_o(n, q) = \arg \max_\tau\ W[e_M(n), \tau, n, q]. \tag{2.8}$$

For given n and q, the political-economy equilibrium τ is constant over time, so that the time subscript t is suppressed henceforth. As τ_{t+1} is exogenous in period t, we likewise drop it from the arguments of W.

As indicated, $\tau_o(n, q)$ is implicitly defined by the first-order condition

$$\frac{\partial W[e_M(n), \tau, n, q]}{\partial \tau} = B[\tau, n, q] = 0, \tag{2.9}$$

and the second-order condition is

$$\frac{\partial^2 W[e_M(n), \tau_0(n, q), n, q]}{\partial \tau^2} = B[\tau_0(n, q), n, q] \le 0, \tag{2.10}$$

where the B_τ is the partial derivative of B with respect to its first argument.

Recalling equation (2.5), we can see that $B(\tau, n, q)$ depends on whether the median voter is skilled or unskilled:

$B(\tau, n, q)$

$$
= \begin{cases}
-w[1 - e_M(n)] + \dfrac{w(1+n)}{(2+n)} l[e^*(\tau, q)] + \dfrac{\gamma\tau(1+n)g[e^*(\tau, q)]}{(2+n)(1-\tau)} \dfrac{\partial e^*}{\partial \tau}, \\
\quad \text{if } e_M(n) < e^*(\tau, q) \\[2mm]
-wq + \dfrac{w(1+n)}{(2+n)} l[e^*(\tau, q)] + \dfrac{\gamma\tau(1+n)g[e^*(\tau, q)]}{(2+n)(1-\tau)} \dfrac{\partial e^*}{\partial \tau} \\
\quad \text{if } e_M(n) > e^*(\tau, q),
\end{cases}
$$

(2.11)

where

$$
l[e^*(\tau, q)] = \int_0^{e^*(\tau, q)} (1 - e)\, dG + q\{1 - G[e^*(\tau, q)]\},
$$

and, by equation (2.1),

$$
\frac{\partial e^*}{\partial \tau} = -\frac{\gamma}{(1-\tau)^2 w} < 0.
$$

The interpretation of expression (2.11) is straightforward. B measures the effect of a rise in the tax rate on the lifetime (that is, $\partial W / \partial \tau$) of the median voter (or more generally, on any individual). The first term in the expression for B is the direct effect caused by the additional tax payment. It is equal to either $-w(1-e)$ or $-wq$, depending on whether the individual is skilled or unskilled, and it is naturally negative. The next two terms measure the indirect effect generated by the increase in the transfer (that is, b) that is made possible by the increase in the tax rate. This indirect effect is decompossed into two terms. The first of these two terms—the second term on the right-hand side of equation (2.11)—reflects the increase in the tax revenues that would occur had the tax base (or

e^*) not changed. This term is always positive: a higher tax rate on a fixed tax base increases revenues. The remaining term reflects the decrease in tax revenues, induced by the reduction in the tax base that is caused by the higher tax rate. In essence, this is the distortionary effect caused by the tax. It is negative, as $\partial e^* / \partial \tau < 0$.

One can also relate the welfare-state-equilibrium tax rate $\tau_o(n, q)$ to the difference between median income (I_M) and average income (I_A), as predicted by the standard models of the determinants of the size of government. (Note that this difference is related to the skewness of the income distribution.) For example, in the case where the median voter is an unskilled worker, $B(\tau, n) = 0$ in the second part of equation (2.11) implies

$$I_M = \frac{\partial(\tau I_A)}{\partial \tau}$$

or

$$\tau \frac{\partial I_A}{\partial \tau} = I_M - I_A, \tag{2.12}$$

where $I_M = wq$ is the pretax median wage and $I_A = l(e^*)/(2 + n)$ is the pretax average taxable income. When there is no income inequality—the limiting case where there are no old, G is concentrated around its mean, and hence $I_M = I_A$—the equilibrium tax rate is zero because there can be no protax coalition. Because the median income is typically smaller than the average income ($I_M - I_A < 0$) and because a labor tax is detrimental to labor supply and pretax labor income (that is, $\partial I_A / \partial \tau < 0$), it follows that the equilibrium tax rate is positive (see also Meltzer and Richard, 1981).[7]

2.3   The Effect of Aging

In this section, we examine the effect of aging on the welfare-state equilibrium. In our model, the share of the elderly in the population is $N_0(1+n)^{t-1}/[N_0(1+n)^{t-1}+N_0(1+n)^t] = 1/(2+n)$. That is, the share of the elderly is inversely related to the population growth rate n. Aging usually means a process where this share rises over time with a variety of dynamic patterns. In this section, we assume that the number of current young fell relative to the number of current old. This means that we assume that a fall in n took place one period before the present. As explained above, there is no correlation between policies across periods (because factor prices are exogenous by the small-country assumption). Therefore, it does not matter whether the change in n that we assumed was anticipated or not. Therefore, our analysis is relevant to the reality of an anticipated, persistent aging of the population.[8]

Total differentiation of equation (2.9) with respect to n implies

$$\frac{\partial \tau_0(n,q)}{\partial n} = -\frac{B_n[\tau_0(n,q),n,q]}{B_\tau[\tau_0(n,q),n,q]}, \tag{2.13}$$

where B_n is the partial derivative of B with respect to its second argument. Because $B_\tau[\tau_0(n,q),n,q] \leq 0$ [see equation (2.10)], it follows that the direction of the effect of changes in n on the equilibrium tax rate τ_0 is determined by the sign of $B_n[\tau_0(n,q),n,q]$.

By differentiating equation (2.11) with respect to n, we conclude that

$$B_n[\tau_0(n,q),n,q]$$

$$= \begin{cases} w\dfrac{de_M}{dn} + wl\{e^*[\tau_0(n,q),q]\}\dfrac{1}{(2+n)^2} + \tau\dfrac{\gamma}{(1-\tau)}\dfrac{g\{e^*[\tau_0(n,q),q]\}}{(2+n)^2}\dfrac{\partial e^*}{\partial \tau} \\[2mm] \quad \text{if } e_M < e^*[\tau_0(n,q),q] \\[4mm] wl\{e^*[\tau_0(n,q),q]\}\dfrac{1}{(2+n)^2} + \tau\dfrac{\gamma}{(1-\tau)}\dfrac{g\{e^*[\tau_0(n,q),q]\}}{(2+n)^2}\dfrac{\partial e^*}{\partial \tau} \\[2mm] \quad \text{if } 1 > e_M > e^*[\tau_0(n,q)], \end{cases}$$

$$\tag{2.14}$$

where

$$\frac{de_M}{dn} = -\frac{1}{2g(e_M)(1+n)^2} < 0,$$

by equation (2.7).

If the sign of $B_n[\tau_0(n,q), n, q]$ is positive, then aging (namely, a decline in n) lowers the political-economy-equilibrium tax rate τ_o and, consequently, the amount of the per-capita transfer b.[9] On inspection of the right-hand side of equation (2.14), we can see that it contains one term—$wl\{e^*[\tau_0(n,q), q]\}/(2+n)^2$—that is positive, whereas the other terms are negative (because de_M/dn and $\partial e^*/\partial \tau$ are both negative). Thus, the sign of $B_n[\tau_0(n,q), n, q]$ cannot be determined a priori. When this is positive, aging of the population (namely, a decrease in n) lowers the political-economy-equilibrium tax rate and the per-capita transfer.

The rationale for this result is as follows. Consider for concreteness the case in which the median voter is a young, skilled individual ($e_M \leq e^*$), and suppose that the population growth rate (which is inversely related to aging) rises. In this case, there is a decline in the amount of tax revenue collected from the median voter that "leaks" to the retirees, who with the higher n become a smaller share of the population. This leakage term—that is, $w\ell(e^*)/(2+n)^2$—is unambiguously a protax factor. However, the median voter now becomes more able (because $de_M/dn < 0$) and therefore opts for a lower tax and transfer. Moreover, the per-capita marginal-efficiency cost of distortionary taxation,

$$\tau\frac{\gamma}{(1-\tau)}\frac{g\{e^*[\tau_0(n,q), q]\}}{(2+n)^2}\frac{\partial e^*}{\partial \tau},$$

rises as well, as can be seen in the last terms on the right-hand sides of equations (2.11) and (2.14).[10] This is also an antitax factor. When the negative terms de_M/dn and $\partial e^*/\partial \tau$ are sufficiently small, the protax factor dominates the antitax factors, and $\partial \tau_0/\partial n$ is positive. In this case, a higher population-growth rate raises the political-economy-equilibrium tax rate and per-capita transfer. Conversely,

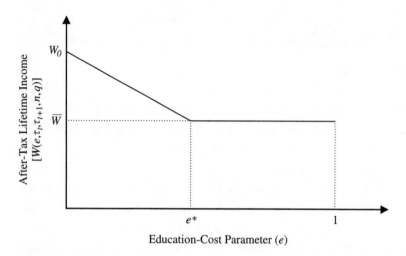

Figure 2.1
After-tax lifetime-income (W) distribution, by education-cost parameter (e)
Notes:
a. The parameters τ_t, τ_{t+1}, n and q are fixed.

b. $W_0 \equiv W(0, \tau_t, \tau_{t+1}, n, q) = (1 - \tau)w - \gamma + b(\tau_t, n, q) + \dfrac{b(\tau_{t+1}, n, q)}{1 + \tau}$

c. $\overline{W} \equiv W(e, \tau_t, \tau_{t+1}, n, q)$ for $e \geq e^*(\tau_t)$

$\quad = (1 - \tau)wq + b(\tau_t, n, q) + \dfrac{b(\tau_{t+1}, n, q)}{1 + \tau}$

aging of the population lowers the political-economy-equilibrium tax rate and transfer.

If the median voter is an unskilled worker, $B_n[\tau_0(n, q), n, q]$ does not include the antitax term de_M/dn because the change in the median voter toward a less able individual is of no consequence, as all of the unskilled have the same demand for redistribution, regardless of their cost-of-education parameter (see figure 2.1).[11] If, furthermore, the distortionary element

$$\tau \frac{\gamma}{(1 - \tau)} \frac{g\{e^*[\tau_0(n, q), q]\}}{(2 + n)^2} \frac{\partial e^*}{\partial \tau}$$

is sufficiently small and q is large enough, then $B_n[\tau_0(n, q), n, q]$ is positive.[12] It then follows that aging of the population lowers the political-economy-equilibrium tax rate and the per-capita transfer, τ and b.

We have so far assumed that $n > 0$, so that the median voter is a member of the working-age population. For completeness, we will also consider briefly the case in which the median voter is among the retired population. In our setup, this happens when $n < 0$. We can see from equation (2.6) that the political-economy-equilibrium tax rate in this case maximizes the transfer, $b(\tau, n, q)$, because retirees' savings from the previous period are already determined. In contrast, when the median voter was a member of the working-age population, the political-economy-equilibrium tax rate maximizes $b(\tau, n, q)$ plus another term, which is after-tax (τ) labor income. This term—either $(1 - \tau)w(1 - e_M)$ or $(1 - \tau)wq$—is decreasing in τ. Thus, the political-economy-equilibrium tax rate "jumps" upward when the old become a majority—that is, as n switches from being positive to being negative.

This effect is along the lines of the theory of Alan H. Meltzer and Scott F. Richard (1981), who attribute the increase in the size of the welfare state to the spread of the right to vote (franchise), which increased the number of voters who have relatively low income and thus a natural incentive to vote for higher taxes and transfers. The increase in the number of social security recipients has an expansionary effect similar to the extension of the franchise in expanding the size of the welfare state. Meltzer and Richard (1981, p. 924) conclude that "In recent years, the proportion of voters receiving social security has increased, raising the number of voters favoring taxes on wage and salary income to finance redistribution. In our analysis the increase in social security recipients has an effect similar to an extension of the franchise." However, if the median voter is not among the retirees—as is probably still the case in all Western countries—then the increased size of the nonworking population may well lead to lower taxes and transfers, as the median voter is adversely affected because she is a net contributor to the welfare system.

2.4   The Effect of the Wage Gap

We now turn to examine the effect of a widening in the wage gap on welfare-state equilibrium. Such a change can be formulated in a variety of ways. For instance, it may take the form of a decline in q. Indeed, this will widen the wage gap, but at the same time it also reduces the average skill (productivity) in the economy because low-skill workers become less productive, whereas the productivity of high-skill workers remains unchanged. However, this is not the experience of the 1990s in which the gap widened because of skill-biased technical changes. We therefore assume that high-skill workers' productivity rises, whereas the productivity of low-skill workers remains unchanged.

Specifically, we denote the productivity of low-skill workers by q_1 and that of high-skill workers by q_2, where naturally $q_1 < q_2$. Hence, the cutoff cost-of-education parameter now becomes

$$e^* = 1 - \frac{q_1}{q_2} - \frac{\gamma}{(1-\tau)q_2 w}. \qquad (2.1')$$

We wish to sign $\partial \tau_0(n, q_1, q_2)/\partial q_2$.

Following the same procedure as in the preceding section, we find that this derivative is now

$$\frac{\partial \tau_0(n, q_1, q_2)}{\partial q_2} = -\frac{B_{q_2}[\tau_0(n, q_1, q_2), n, q_1, q_2]}{B_\tau[\tau_0(n, q_1, q_2), n, q_1, q_2]}, \qquad (2.15)$$

where B_{q_2} is the partial derivative of B with respect to q_2.

Because $B_\tau \leqq 0$ [see condition (2.10)], it follows that the sign of $\partial \tau_0/\partial q_2$ is equal to the sign of B_{q_2}. This derivative is found from equation (2.11). For the sake of simplicity, assume that e is uniformly distributed over the interval $[0, 1]$. In this case, we have

$$\ell[e^*(\tau,q_1,q_2)] = q_2 e^*(\tau,q_1,q_2) - \frac{1}{2}q_2[e^*(\tau,q_1,q_2)]^2 + [1 - e^*(\tau,q_1,q_2)]q_1$$

and

$$g(e) = 1.$$

Therefore, equation (2.11) becomes

$$B(\tau,n,q_1,q_2)$$

$$= \begin{cases} -wq_2(1 - e_M) + \dfrac{w(1+n)}{(2+n)}\ell[e^*(\tau,q_1,q_2)] - \dfrac{\tau(1+n)\gamma^2}{(2+n)(1-\tau)^3 wq_2} \\ \quad \text{if } e_M(n) < e^*(\tau,q_1,q_2) \\ -wq_1 + \dfrac{w(1+n)}{(2+n)}\ell[e^*(\tau,q_1,q_2)] - \dfrac{\tau(1+n)\gamma^2}{(2+n)(1-\tau)^3 wq_2} \\ \quad \text{if } e_M(n) > e^*(\tau,q_1,q_2). \end{cases}$$

$$(2.11')$$

As in the preceding section, the expression for B (which is the effect of a change in the tax rate on lifetime income) consists of three terms: the first term is the direct effect caused by the higher tax payments, and it is negative; the second term reflects the change in the transfer had the tax base remained constant, and it is positive; and the last term measures the distortionary effect (the change in the tax base), and it is negative.

Differentiating equation (2.11') with respect to q_2 yields

$$B_{q_2} = \begin{cases} -w(1 - e_M) + \dfrac{w(1+n)}{2+n}\dfrac{\partial\ell}{\partial q_2} + \dfrac{\tau(1+n)\gamma^2}{(2+n)(1-\tau)^3 q_2^2} & \text{if } e_M < e^* \\ 0 + \dfrac{w(1+n)}{2+n}\dfrac{\partial\ell}{\partial q_2} + \dfrac{\tau(1+n)\gamma^2}{(2+n)(1-\tau)^3 q_2^2} & \text{if } e_M < e^*, \end{cases}$$

$$(2.16)$$

where $\partial\ell/\partial q_2 > 0$ (that is, as expected, an increase in the productivity of high-skill workers increases the effective labor supply). The difference between the case of a skilled median voter and an un-skilled median voter is that B_{q_2} contains a term $-w(1 - e_M) < 0$ in the first case. This term reflects the fact that an increase in the tax rate is more painful to a skilled median voter when her productivity rises. The other two terms are positive because an increase in the tax rate generates a higher increase in the transfer when q_2 rises. This follows because the distortionary effect (the third term) becomes less important when q_2 rises: the nondeductibility of the pecuniary cost of education γ, which is the source of the distortion, becomes less relevant when the return to education rises following the in-crease in q_2. Thus, we conclude that $\partial \tau_0 / \partial q_2$ is positive (that is, the equilibrium tax rate rises as the wage gap widens) when the median voter is unskilled. On the other hand, $\partial \tau_0 / \partial q_2$ could well be negative or negligible (that is, the equilibrium tax rate falls as the wage gap widens), when the median voter is skilled.

2.5   Some Empirical Evidence

We next use data for the United States and ten European countries over the period 1965 through 1996 to examine the relationship be-tween tax rates and benefits on the one hand and the dependency ratio and the wage gap on the other.[13] We estimate regressions in which the dependent variables of the labor tax rate and real per-capita transfers are functions of the return to education (a proxy for the wage gap), the share of the population with high education (a proxy for the skill of the median voter), the dependency ratio (which is positively related to the aging of the population), and ad-ditional control variables. These include a measure of income distri-bution suggested by previous theories that seek to explain the size of the welfare state (e.g., Meltzer and Richard, 1981; Persson and Tabellini, 2002), government employment as a share of total em-ployment to indicate the breadth of government involvement in the economy, real gross domestic product (GDP) growth to control for business-cycle effects, and a measure of openness to trade to capture exposure to external shocks against which the welfare state might provide social insurance (as in Rodrik, 1998).

Data on the labor-tax rate from 1965 to 1992 are from Enrique Mendoza, Assaf Razin, and Linda Tesar (1994), as extended by Mendoza, Gian Maria Milesi-Ferretti, and Patrick Asea (1997), and Francesco Daveri and Guido Tabellini (2000); these are derived by using revenue statistics to calculate an average tax rate on labor income. A brief description on how these tax rates are calculated is provided in the appendix to chapter 6. The measure of income distribution is derived from Klaus Deininger and Lyn Squire (1996), who provides measures of income shares by quintile over time, with missing observations obtained through linear interpolation. The regressions use the ratio of the income share of the top quintile to the combined share of the middle three quintiles; this is the "skewness" of income distribution (Meltzer and Richard, 1981).

The measures of the return to higher education are from OECD (1998) and are for women completing the upper level of secondary school in 1995 (results for men are similar). This is the internal rate of return, which equates the present value of higher lifetime income as a result of more education to the present value of the opportunity cost of attaining it. The share of the population by educational attainment is from Robert J. Barro and Jong-Wha Lee (2002), with values between five-year benchmarks obtained through linear interpolation. Note that our theory indicates that the effect of the wage gap on the equilibrium tax rate depends on the interaction between the return to education and the share of individuals with high education. The interaction of these variables is thus used in the regressions. This is useful in the empirical specification since our measure of the return to education varies only across countries and not over time.

The OECD Analytical Database is used to calculate measures of real per-capita GDP growth, per-capita transfers received by

households, government employment as a share of total employment, and openness to trade defined as the sum of the imports plus
exports as a share of GDP. The dependency rate is defined as one
minus the labor force as a share of the population. Per-capita transfers include both social security and other transfers such as unemployment and disability compensation, though social security is by
far the largest component of transfers in all countries. Transfers are
deflated by each country's Consumer Price Index (CPI) to provide
real transfers in 1990 terms and then translated into the common
currency of U.S. dollars.

Table 2.1 provides results from ordinary-least-squares (OLS) regressions for the determinant of the labor-tax rate and (log) real
transfers per capita. All specifications include a complete set of

Table 2.1
Determinants of the Labor-Tax Rate and Social Transfers (274 observations)

Independent Variable	Dependent Variable: Labor-Tax Rate		Dependent Variable: Social Transfers	
	(1)	(2)	(3)	(4)
(Return to education) × (High-education share)		0.895 (3.41)		9.098 (4.54)
Dependency rate	−0.466 (−4.61)	−0.159 (−1.19)	−8.409 (−10.73)	−5.290 (−5.18)
Government jobs per employment	0.838 (10.18)	0.816 (10.08)	3.519 (5.52)	3.294 (5.34)
Trade openness	0.225 (6.49)	0.210 (6.12)	0.533 (1.98)	0.378 (1.44)
Per-capita GDP growth	−0.292 (−3.23)	−0.236 (−2.62)	−2.814 (−4.02)	−2.251 (−3.28)
Income skewedness	−0.006 (−0.33)	−0.015 (−0.87)	0.423 (3.06)	0.326 (2.42)
R^2	0.684	0.698	0.623	0.651

Note: All specifications include country fixed effects (coefficients not shown). The *t*
statistics are in parentheses.

country fixed effects. Columns (1) and (2) show results for the labor-tax rate, and columns (3) and (4) those for per-capita real transfers. In both cases, the interaction of the return to education and the share of the highly educated in the population has a positive and strongly significant coefficient. This is consistent with our theoretical model: the less educated are the majority in all countries and would thus be expected to favor higher taxes and transfers as either the share of the education rises (but remains still a minority) or the return to education increases. The positive coefficient of the interaction term is driven by the share of the educated in the population. This variable by itself is positive and statistically significant, and the interaction with the return to education is not significant when both are included in the regression (this is not surprising since we have only one observation per country for the return to education). In table 2.1 the influence of the return to education by itself is captured by the country fixed effects. The dependency rate has a statistically significant negative effect on the labor-tax rate and transfers. The young are the majority of the population and thus would naturally vote for lower taxes and transfers as the number of dependents goes up to limit the "fiscal leakage" from the welfare state.[14]

The results for the other variables are sensible and are qualitatively unchanged in adding the interacted education variable. A larger share of government employment is associated with a higher tax rate and more transfers, while countries more open to trade have larger welfare states, as predicted by Rodrik (1998). However, the effect of the trade-openness (globalization) variable is hard to assess. In a slightly different sample and with another explanatory variable (migration), the coefficient of this variable loses its significance and even changes its sign (see table 2.2 below). The significant negative coefficient for per-capita real GDP growth is in line with the use of automatic stabilizers providing countercyclical fiscal policy. The coefficient on the income-skewedness variable is not statistically significant for tax rates but is positive and significant for transfers. This matches the prediction of previous theories that inequality leads to pressure for redistribution.

2.6 Low-Skill Migration: Theory and Evidence

We found that aging of the population may induce counter-intuitively lower tax rates and benefits. A key explanation for such a result is a sort of fiscal leakage from the median voter to the elderly, who are net beneficiaries of the welfare state (because they pay no labor taxes and receive benefits). A similar mechanism is at work in the case of low-skill immigration. We find that a higher share of unskilled migrants in the population may actually reduce the size of the welfare state (that is, τ and b), if they are integrated into the welfare system—namely, if they pay taxes and qualify for transfers. This result holds even when these unskilled migrants are allowed to participate in the voting process.

The formal derivation of this result can be found in Razin, Sadka, and Swagel (2002a). Here we explain only the rationale for this result. There are two conflicting effects of migration on taxation and redistribution. On the one hand, low-income migrants who are net beneficiaries from the tax-transfer system join forces with the native-born, low-income voters in favor of higher taxes and transfers. Put differently, low-skill migration induces a shift in the median voter toward the bottom end of the skill distribution (higher e_M). On the other hand, redistribution becomes more costly to the native-born population as the migrants share some of the benefits at their expense. This is the fiscal leakage (from the median voter to the migrants) effect. As the number of migrants grows, a larger proportion of the tax revenues actually ends up in the hands of low-skill migrants. Therefore, the native-born taxpayers, including the median voter, will opt now for lower taxes. This shift in the general attitude of the native-born taxpayers against high taxes may be larger than the effect of the shift in the median voter. Therefore, a larger share of low-skill migrants may actually lower rather than raise the political-economy-equilibrium tax rate and benefit. This result is evidently reinforced by the low voting-participation rate among low-skill migrants.[15]

The following empirical evidence sheds some light on these theoretical considerations. We use data for eleven European countries (the ten countries included in the data set of the preceding section and Austria) over the period 1974 through 1992. We used identical regressors in regressions for the determinants of the labor-tax rate and the log of social transfers per capita in real dollars. The baseline specification includes the share of government jobs, the dependency ratio, trade openness, per-capita GDP growth, the measure of income skewedness suggested by the standard theory (rich per middle), and the share of income for the poor relative to the middle. All regressions include country fixed effects.

Table 2.2 contains results for the determinants of the tax rate on labor income. Column (1) shows results without any variable for immigration. The tax rate on labor income is positively and significantly related to the involvement of the government in the economy as measured by the share of government jobs. In contrast, the measures of income distribution are both far from significant, and there is likewise little support for the hypothesis that the welfare state exists to provide social insurance against external shocks. The coefficient on the dependency ratio is negative and highly significant as suggested in the preceding sections.

The remaining columns of table 2.2 add data on the stock of immigrants as a share of the population to the base specification, first for the share of all immigrants and then for immigrants by education level. In column (2), the share of immigrants out of the population has a negative sign (suggesting that fiscal-leakage effects dominate the shift in the median voter), though this coefficient is significant at only the 23 percent confidence level. One

Table 2.2
Determinants of the Tax Rate on Labor Income (dependent variable: labor-tax rate, 146 observations)

	Regression Equation				
	(1)	(2)	(3)	(4)	(5)
Government jobs per total employment	0.879 (7.34)	0.877 (7.34)	0.620 (4.65)	0.901 (8.75)	0.699 (5.52)
Dependency ratio	−1.168 (−7.59)	−1.287 (−7.05)	−1.358 (−7.76)	−1.185 (−6.96)	−1.254 (−7.53)
Trade openness	−0.003 (−0.10)	−0.004 (−0.16)	−0.045 (−1.65)	0.008 (0.34)	−0.026 (−0.99)
Per-capita GDP growth	−0.015 (−0.25)	−0.035 (−0.55)	−0.006 (−0.10)	0.027 (0.45)	0.042 (0.72)
Rich per middle-income share	−0.009 (−0.18)	−0.033 (−0.62)	−0.019 (−0.37)	−0.033 (−0.68)	−0.022 (−0.47)
Poor per middle-income share	−0.065 (−0.040)	−0.101 (−0.61)	−0.059 (−0.38)	−0.017 (−0.11)	0.006 (0.04)
Unemployment rate			0.327 (3.73)		0.259 (3.07)
Immigrants per population		−0.403 (−1.20)	−0.614 (−1.89)	−10.852 (−4.88)	−9.723 (−4.45)
Medium- + high-education immigrants per population				19.043 (4.75)	16.679 (8.37)
R^2	0.652	0.656	0.690	0.708	0.728

Note: All specifications include country fixed effects (coefficients not shown). The t statistics are in parentheses.

percentage-point increase in the share of immigrants in the population (a roughly 20 percent increase in the total stock of immigrants of all eleven countries) leads to a 0.4 percentage-point decline in the labor-tax rate. The other results are essentially unchanged with the immigrant share added to the regression.

There is a positive relationship between the unemployment rate and the labor-tax rate. As suggested by Daveri and Tabellini (2000), this possibly reflects the effects in the other direction of high labor taxes leading to high unemployment in Europe. With the unemployment rate added, the coefficient on the share of immigrants becomes more negative and significant at the 5 percent confidence level.

Column (4) shows the baseline specification with immigrants separated by education level. The results are consistent with our theory: low-education immigrants have a statistically significant negative effect on the tax rate, while the combined category of medium- and high-education immigrants has a significant and positive effect. The results are unchanged in column (5), where the unemployment rate is again added. The composition of immigrants thus matters for the tax rate in a way that is consistent with the model: low-education immigrants lead to lower taxes, whereas an increased share of medium- and high-education immigrants, who would likely not be net recipients of government benefits, leads to higher tax rates.[16] Immigration might also increase income inequality and thus lead to higher taxes, as predicted by the standard theory (although our empirical results are inconclusive on this point because the coefficient on the variable suggested by the standard theory, while negative, is not statistically significant), but our results show that immigration has an independent effect on tax rates, and this independent effect works to reduce taxes, as is consistent with our theory.

Table 2.3 shows results for the determinants of social transfers per person (in the common currency of real dollars). As with the labor-tax rate, the share of government jobs has a significant positive effect on social transfers, whereas the dependency ratio has a significant negative effect. In contrast to the result for the tax rate, the coefficients on both measures of income distribution are significant. However, the variable for income skewedness suggested by the standard theory has the wrong sign, with greater inequality leading to lower rather than higher redistribution. On the other hand, the negative coefficient on the poor-per-middle variable indicates that greater inequality leads to more generous transfers.

Table 2.3
Determinants of Per-Capita Social Transfers (dependent variable: social transfers per capita in real dollars, 146 observations)

	Regression Equation				
	(1)	(2)	(3)	(4)	(5)
Government jobs per total employment	4.359 (3.13)	4.461 (3.65)	5.263 (3.69)	4.618 (3.84)	5.825 (4.14)
Dependency ratio	−10.247 (−5.72)	−3.908 (−2.09)	−3.685 (−1.96)	−3.346 (−1.81)	−2.941 (−1.59)
Trade openness	−2.028 (−6.73)	−1.946 (−7.35)	−1.819 (−6.29)	−1.879 (−7.19)	−1.682 (−5.87)
Per-capita GDP growth	−1.388 (−1.95)	−0.336 (−0.52)	−0.425 (−6.25)	0.009 (0.01)	−0.078 (−0.12)
Rich per middle-income share	−2.399 (−4.22)	−1.115 (−2.07)	−1.159 (−2.15)	−1.117 (−2.11)	−1.181 (−2.24)
Poor per middle-income share	−7.350 (−3.89)	−5.424 (−3.21)	−5.554 (−3.29)	−4.959 (2.97)	−5.090 (−3.07)
Unemployment rate			−1.022 (−1.09)		−.514 (−1.62)
Immigrants per population		21.583 (6.30)	22.244 (6.39)	−36.328 (−1.51)	−42.945 (−1.77)
Medium- + high-education immigrants per population				105.532 (2.43)	119.375 (2.71)
R^2	0.497	0.616	0.620	0.633	0.641

Note: All specifications include country fixed effects (coefficients not shown). The *t* statistics are in parentheses.

The coefficient on GDP growth is also significant in contrast to the results for the labor-tax rate, suggesting a countercyclical role for social transfers (however, this coefficient is not statistically significant in the other specifications for transfers).

Adding the stock of immigrants out of the population in column (2) gives a strong positive effect of immigrants on transfers—the opposite that was found for the tax rate. To put this in perspective, average social transfers rose from $2,300 in 1984 to $4,500 in 1991 (in real 1990 dollars), a change of 0.8 in logs. Over this period, the share of immigrants in the population rose from just over 3.5 percent to not quite 4.4 percent. Multiplying this 0.8 percentage-point change by the coefficient of 21.6 for the share of immigrants in column (2) indicates that the rising share of immigrants accounts for more than 20 percent of rising benefits (0.18 of the 0.8 log change in benefits). The results for the other variables are qualitatively unchanged, though the coefficient on GDP growth is no longer significant, and the magnitudes of coefficients on the dependency ratio and the income-distribution variables change somewhat. It is interesting as well that the fit of the transfers regression (the within-country R^2) improves markedly with the addition of the stock of immigrants, from 0.5 to better than 0.6, in contrast to the tax regression, where this hardly mattered. The results are essentially unchanged with the inclusion of the unemployment rate in column (3).

Separating immigrants by education in columns (4) and (5) of table 2.3 provides results that are more in line with those for the labor-tax rate in table 2.2. As before, rising social transfers are related to medium- and high-education immigrants for which the coefficients in both columns are statistically significant, while there are negative but not as strongly significant coefficients on the overall share of immigrants in the population (thus on the low-skilled immigrants).

It is worth mentioning the negative and significant coefficient of the trade-openness (globalization) explanatory variable in all of the five regressions for the per-capita social transfer (see table 2.3). This is in contrast to the safety-net hypothesis of Rodrik. Note that this explanatory variable has an insignificant role for the labor-tax rate (see table 2.2). We conjecture here that because trade openness goes hand in hand with capital-account openness, then the trade-openness coefficient may actually capture the effect of capital-account openness. Globalization that stimulates tax competition among governments with respect to capital income leads to low capital-income-tax rates and revenues, thereby forcing a decline in the per-capita transfers. We return to this issue in part 2.

Finally, there is a potential problem of reverse causality from the tax rate and benefits to the immigrant share. First, if taxes affect migration, this would likely *strengthen* our results. This is because higher taxes or benefits would be expected to lead to more immigration of low-skilled workers (with higher-education immigrants moving for reasons other than benefits). But this means that in our regressions, this positive effect of taxes or benefits on immigration is partially offsetting the negative effect we find of migration on taxes (or covering up a negative effect of migration on benefits). However, it is also possible that countries with more elaborate welfare systems will choose to tighten their migration quotas, especially with respect to unskilled migrants. This can offer an alternative explanation for the negative correlation between the tax rate and migration share that we find in the data.

2.7   Conclusion

The demand for redistribution by the decisive voter is affected by the growing demands on the welfare state's public finances implied by an aging population, low-skill migration, and widening wage gaps. Both an aging population and low-skill migration have similar effects on the political-economy-equilibrium tax rates and transfers.

On the one hand, an aging population or a higher share of low-skill migrants means a larger protax coalition because the retired and low-skill migrants are net beneficiaries of transfers from those who are employed. On the other hand, an aging population or a higher share of low-skill migrants puts a higher tax burden on the people around the median voter because it is necessary to finance transfers to a larger share of the population (a fiscal-leakage effect). People for whom the costs of higher taxes outweigh benefits shift to the antitax coalition. Hence, it may well be the case that the second factor dominates and the political-economy-equilibrium tax rate declines when the dependency ratio or the share of low-skill migrants rises. The effect of a widening wage gap on the political-economy-equilibrium tax and benefit depends on whether the median voter is skilled or not: when she is skilled, the tax rate and the benefit decline; the opposite is true when she is not skilled. These hypotheses are supported by our empirical analysis.

3   Migration and the
           Welfare State

3.1 Introduction

As is discussed in the preceding chapter, low-skill migration
may downscale the welfare state because of a fiscal-leakage effect,
and high-skill migration may boost the welfare state because of a
fiscal-injection effect. In this chapter, we examine the theory behind
a converse hypothesis—namely, whether the welfare state attracts
low-skill migrants and does not attract high-skill migrants.

3.2 Low-Skill Migration

We simplify the human-capital-formation model of the preceding
chapter by deleting features that are inessential to the study of what
determines the flow of migration. Because aging is not the focus in
this chapter, we also reduce the dynamic overlapping-generations
model into a static one-period model. Also, because we wish to
study only whether the welfare state is attractive to migration and
not the determination of tax rates and benefits of the welfare state,
we assume away the distortions caused by taxation on the forma-
tion of human capital. Recall that in the presence of taxes the pecuniary cost γ of acquiring skill was the element through which the
distortion manifested itself. We therefore now eliminate γ.

In this setup, the tax has no effect on the decision to acquire skill. The cutoff ability level (e^*) between acquiring and not acquiring skill is given by the following equation:

$$e^* = 1 - q. \tag{3.1}$$

Denote the disposable income of an e individual by $w(e)$. This is equal to

$$W(e) = \begin{cases} (1 - \tau)w(1 - e) + [1 + (1 - \tau)r]K + b & \text{for } e \leq e^* \\ (1 - \tau)qw + [1 + (1 - \tau)r]K + b & \text{for } e \geq e^*, \end{cases} \tag{3.2}$$

as we assume that each individual is born with K units of capital. The tax rate τ applies also to capital income, as this source of income distinguishes the native-born individuals from the migrants, who are assumed to possess no capital.

As in the preceding chapter, the disposable-income-distribution curve is piece-wise linear in the cost-of-education parameter e. This refers to the native-born population. For individuals who do not acquire skill (those with a cost-of-education parameter e above the cutoff parameter e^*), the cost-of-education parameter is irrelevant, and they have the same income. Naturally, within the group of individuals who do decide to become skilled (that is, for $e \leq e^*$), the more able the individual is (that is, the lower e is), then the higher her disposable income is. As can be seen from equation (3.2), this relationship is linear. The income-distribution curve is depicted in figure 3.1. Note that the slope of the downward-sloping segment is $-(1 - \tau)w$. Also, notice that e^* is unaffected by the income-distribution policy (namely, τ and b). We assume that the migrants (whose number is m) are all unskilled and possess no physical capital. Their disposable income is only $(1 - \tau)qw + b$, which is below that of the unskilled native-born individuals.

We assume a standard (concave, constant-returns-to-scale) production function[1]

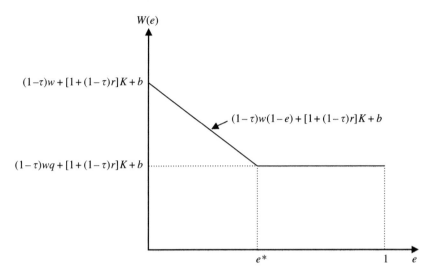

Figure 3.1
The income-distribution curve

$$Y = F(K, L), \tag{3.3}$$

where Y is gross output, K is the total stock of capital (recall that
each individual possesses K units of capital and the number of individuals is normalized to one), and L is the supply of labor, which is
given by

$$L = \int_0^{e^*} (1 - e)\, dG + q[1 - G(e^*)] + qm. \tag{3.4}$$

The wage rate and the gross rental price of capital are given in a
competitive equilibrium by the marginal productivity conditions

$$w = F_L(K, L) \tag{3.5}$$

and

$$1 + r = F_K(K, L), \tag{3.6}$$

where F_i is the partial derivative of F with respect to $i = K, L$, and
we continue to assume 100 percent depreciation.

The income-tax parameters τ and b are related to each other by the government budget constraint

$$b(1 + m) = \tau(Y - K). \tag{3.7}$$

Note that the base for the flat income-tax rate is net-of-depreciation domestic product $(Y - K)$, including labor income of migrants that is subject to the income tax. (Recall that capital fully depreciates at the end of the production process.) Also, migrants qualify to the uniform demogrant b.

Finally, there are no barriers to migration, so that m is determined endogeneously by

$$(1 - \tau)qw + b = w^*, \tag{3.8}$$

where w^* is the opportunity income (reservation wage) of the migrants in the source countries.

Consider now the mechanism through which the welfare state indeed attracts migrants. More generally, is it true that more taxes and more transfers attract more migrants in the context of our stylized model? Specifically, we study the sign of $dm/d\tau$.

To simplify the exposition further, we assume a uniform distribution of the ability parameter e over the interval $[0,1]$, so that $G(e) = e$. This assumption yields a simple effective-labor-supply function as follows:

$$L = \frac{1}{2}(1 - q)^2 + q(1 + m), \tag{3.4'}$$

where use is made of equation (3.1).

Substituting equations (3.3), (3.4'), (3.5), (3.6), and (3.8) into equation (3.7) and rearranging terms yields

$$\left\{ w^* - (1 - \tau)qF_L\left[K, \frac{1}{2}(1 - q)^2 + q(1 + m)\right] \right\}(1 + m)$$

$$= \tau\left\{ F\left[K, \frac{1}{2}(1 - q)^2 + q(1 + m)\right] - K \right\}. \tag{3.9}$$

Total differentiation of equation (3.9) with respect to τ yields

$$[w^* - qF_L - (1+m)(1-\tau)q^2F_{LL}]\frac{dm}{d\tau} = F - K - (1+m)qF_L, \qquad (3.10)$$

where F_{LL} is the second-order derivative of F with respect to L.

By substituting equations (3.4'), (3.5), (3.8), and the Euler's equation $F(K,L) = (1+r)K + wL$ into equation (3.10), we conclude that

$$[b - q\tau w - (1+m)(1-\tau)q^2F_{LL}]\frac{dm}{d\tau} = rK + \frac{1}{2}(1-q)^2w. \qquad (3.11)$$

It is straightforward to see from the government budget constraint [namely, equation (3.7)] that the tax on labor income paid by an unskilled individual (namely, τqw) must fall short of her transfer (namely, b), which is $b > \tau qw$. Because $F_{LL} < 0$, it finally follows from equation (3.11) that

$$\frac{dm}{d\tau} > 0. \qquad (3.12)$$

Thus, as expected, more taxes and transfers must attract more unskilled migrants. Inspection of equation (3.11) reveals also some of the undefined parameters that determine the magnitude of this effect.

3.3   The Welfare State and the Skill Mix of Migration

The unambiguous conclusion that the more intensive the welfare state is, the more attractive it becomes to migrants is restricted to the case of low-skill migration. If we allow for high-skill migrants as well, we can examine whether the welfare state attracts more low-skill migrants and fewer high-skill migrants.

Denote the number of low-skill migrants and high-skill migrants by m_ℓ and m_h, respectively. Suppose that their opportunity incomes (reservation wages) in their home countries are w_ℓ^* and w_h^*, respectively. Then the migration equation (3.8) is replaced by two equations, one for each skill type:

$$(1 - \tau)qw + b = w_\ell^* \tag{3.8a}$$

and

$$(1 - \tau)w + b = w_h^*. \tag{3.8b}$$

The effective labor-supply equation (3.4′) becomes now

$$L = \frac{1}{2}(1 - q)^2 + q(1 + m_\ell) + m_h = \frac{1}{2}(1 - q)^2 + q + m_1, \tag{3.4″}$$

where $m_1 \equiv qm_\ell + m_h$ is the labor supply of the migrants in efficiency units. The government's budget constraint [namely, equation (3.7)] now becomes

$$b(1 + m_2) = \tau(Y - K), \tag{3.7′}$$

where $m_2 \equiv m_\ell + m_h$ is the total number of low- and high-skill migrants. Finally, the other equations of the model—namely, equations (3.1), (3.3), (3.5), and (3.6)—remain intact.

We can solve equations (3.8a) and (3.8b) for b and w:[2]

$$b = \frac{w_\ell^* - qw_h^*}{1 - q}, \tag{3.13}$$

and

$$w = \frac{w_h^* - w_\ell^*}{(1 - \tau)(1 - q)}. \tag{3.14}$$

Substituting equations (3.1), (3.4′), and (3.13) into equation (3.7′), we get

$$\left(\frac{w_\ell^* - qw_h^*}{1 - q}\right)(1 + m_2) = \tau\left\{F\left[K, \frac{1}{2}(1 - q)^2 + q + m_1\right] - K\right\}$$

$$\equiv R(\tau, m_1), \tag{3.15}$$

where $R(\tau, m_1)$ is tax revenues. Substituting equations (3.14) and

(3.4″) into equation (3.5) yields

$$w_h^* - w_\ell^* = (1 - \tau)(1 - q)F_L\left[K, \frac{1}{2}(1 - q)^2 + q + m_1\right].\qquad(3.16)$$

The latter two equations [namely, equations (3.15) and (3.16)] can now be solved for the effective labor supply (m_1) and the number (m_2) of the migrants as functions of the tax rate (τ). Total differentiation of equation (3.16) with respect to τ yields

$$\frac{dm_1}{d\tau} = F_L[(1 - \tau)F_{LL}]^{-1} < 0$$

because we assume that the marginal product of labor is diminishing (that is, F is concave). On inspection of equation (3.15), we can see that

$$sign\left(\frac{dm_2}{d\tau}\right) = sign\left(\frac{dR}{d\tau}\right),$$

where $dR/d\tau = \partial R/\partial \tau + (\partial R/\partial m_1)(dm_1/d\tau)$. Suppose that "supply-side economics" does not prevail—that is, $dR/d\tau > 0$—so that an increase in the tax rate must raise tax revenues. (The no-Laffer-curve property is always true for small τ's.) Then, $dm_2/d\tau > 0$.

Thus, we have established that when the tax rate (τ) is raised, the labor supply of migrants (m_1) falls, whereas the number of migrants (m_2) rises. That is,

$$\frac{dm_1}{d\tau} \equiv q\frac{dm_\ell}{d\tau} + \frac{dm_h}{d\tau} < 0,$$

whereas

$$\frac{dm_2}{d\tau} \equiv \frac{dm_\ell}{d\tau} + \frac{dm_h}{d\tau} > 0.$$

This can happen if and only if $dm_\ell/d\tau > 0$ and $dm_h/d\tau < 0$. Therefore, as expected, more taxes and transfers attract more low-skill migrants and fewer high-skill migrants.

3.4   Conclusion

Although low-skill migration may plausibly downscale the welfare state and high-skill migration may boost the welfare state,
a downscaled welfare state attracts fewer low-skill migrants and
more high-skill ones. The two mechanisms may lead to a sort of
joint stable equilibrium of migration and the size of the welfare
state. If the welfare state grows out of this equilibrium, it will attract more low-skill migrants and fewer high-skill migrants. This,
in turn, generates a political-economy response that downscales the
welfare state, going back to the original joint equilibrium. Similarly,
if the welfare state is downscaled out of the equilibrium, then it will
attract fewer low-skill migrants and more high-skill migrants. This,
in turn, generates political forces that boost the size of the welfare,
bringing it back to the original joint equilibrium.

4   Balanced-Budget Rules and the Downscaling of the Welfare State

4.1   Introduction

As is shown in chapter 2, aging can tilt the political-power balance toward downscaling the welfare state. One well-publicized proposal for reducing the size of the welfare state is to shift from national pensions to individual retirement accounts. In this chapter, we examine how rigid balanced-budget rules that do not make exceptions for fundamental structural changes in social security can impede such shifts.

4.2   Social Security versus Individual Retirement Accounts: An Overview

The economic viability of national old-age security systems has been increasingly deteriorating. Though the 2000 population census in the United States reveals some encouraging signs that the aging process is checked through increasing fertility rates and migration of young people, the demographic picture for Europe is cloudy. As vividly put by *The Economist* (2002, p. 23):

As its people grow fewer, Europe's state pensions systems will go deeper into the red. Germany and Italy are trying to push the private-sector alternative. It is not easy.

More concretely, for Germany (*The Economist*, 2002, p. 44):

Seven-tenths of German pensions come from a state scheme with roots in Bismarck's day. It is financed mainly by a levy on wages, 19.1% this year, half paid by workers and half by employers. But, as all over Europe, the demographics are grim. Today, there are 2.8 Germans aged 20–59 to support each pensioner. By 2030 there could be half as many. And the state can't just fork out money to fill the gap.

And similarly, in Italy (*The Economist*, 2002, p. 45):

The government's strategy is to get private pension schemes and funds, now embryonic, working properly first. Then, it hopes, it will be politically able to tackle the financing of the pay-as-you-go state system. But Italy cannot afford to wait. Its state's spending on pensions is more than 14% of GDP, almost double the European Union average. Every year, payouts far exceed contributions by workers and employers.

Indeed, the aging of the population raises the burden of financing the existing pay-as-you-go, national pension (old-age security) systems because relatively falling numbers of workers have to bear the cost of paying pensions to relatively rising numbers of retirees. Against this backdrop, proposals have been made to privatize social security to sustain the existing systems. This, by and large, means a shift away from the current pay-as-you-go systems and toward individual retirement accounts (or fully funded systems). A supposedly added benefit to such a shift is that contributions to individual accounts would produce higher returns than pay-as-you-go national pension systems would produce. If privatized pensions can offer better rates of return than national pensions, the transition from the latter to the former may be smooth. However, a careful scrutiny of the pensions' rate-of-return argument reveals that it is flawed, as neatly demonstrated by Paul Krugman (2002).

We imagine an overlapping-generations model with just one young (working) person and one old (retired) person in each period. Each individual lives for two periods. Suppose that there is a pay-as-you-go national pension system by which the worker contributes one euro to finance the pension benefit of one euro paid to the retiree. Each young person contributes one euro when young and working and receives one euro on retirement. Evidently, the young person earns zero return on her contribution to the national pay-as-you-go, old-age security system. If, instead, the young person were to invest her one euro in an individual account, she would have earned the real market rate of return of, say, 100 percent, allowing her a pension of two euros at retirement. (Recall that the average length of time between the first period of her life, in which she works, and the second period of her life, in which she is a pensioner, could be something like thirty years; so that a real rate of return of 100 percent between these two periods is not exorbitant.) Is the young person better off with this transition from pay-as-you-go systems to individual retirement accounts? If the government still wishes to honor the existing "social contract" (or political norm) to pay a pension benefit of one euro to the old at the time of the transition, the government can issue a debt of one euro. The interest to be paid by the government on this debt at the market rate of 100 percent will be one euro in each period, starting from the next period ad infinitum. Hence the young person will be levied a tax of one euro in the next period (when old) to finance the interest payment. Thus, her net-of tax balance in the individual account will be only one euro, implying a zero net-of-tax return in the individual account—the same return as in the national, pay-as-you-go system. And what if the individual invests the one euro in the equity market and gets a better return than the 100 percent that the government pays on its debt? If the capital markets are efficient, the higher equity return (relative to the government bond rate) reflects nothing but a risk premium. That is, the equity premium is equal to the risk premium through arbitrage. Therefore, equity investment offers no gain in risk-adjusted return over government bonds.[1] And if markets are inefficient, then the government can, as a general policy, issue debt to invest in the equity market, irrespective of the issue of replacing social security by individual retirement accounts.

Nevertheless, the increased fragility of national pay-as-you-go pension systems, caused by the aging of the population, raises doubts among the young about whether the next generations will continue to honor the implicit intergenerational social contract—the political norm, according to which, "I pay now for the pension benefits of the old, and the next young generation pays for my pension benefits when I get old." These doubts are not unfounded, for after all there will indeed be more pensioners per each young worker of the next generation, and hence each one of the young workers will have to pay more to honor the implicit social contract. With such doubts, the political-power balance may indeed shift toward scaling down the pay-as-you-go system, encouraging the establishment of supplemental individual retirement accounts.[2] Such accounts are, by their very nature, fully funded, so that they are not directly affected by the aging of the population.[3] Naturally, the existing old generation opposes any scaling down of the pay-as-you-go system because it stands to lose pension benefits (without enjoying the reduction in the social security contributions). This opposition can, however, be softened or altogether removed if the government creates a budget deficit to support the social security system. By not scaling down the pension benefits to the current old, the government can fully offset the reduction in social security contributions or even maintain these benefits intact. (Of course, this deficit will be carried over to the future, with its debt service smoothed over the next several generations.) However, some self-imposed restrictions (such as those imposed by the Stability and Growth Pact in the European Union, which put a ceiling on the current fiscal deficit), may stand in the way. As put by Guido Tabellini (2003, p. 83),

The current formulation of the Stability and Growth Pact is problematic ... The Pact now emphasizes the budget deficit, but neglects the longer-term generational imbalances. For instance, consider a pension reform that gradually but permanently reduces pension outlays in the future, but immediately cuts social security contributions so as to relax political constraints. A transition from a pay-as-you-go towards a fully-funded private pension system could have this effect. Such a reform could run against the Stability Pact as currently formulated, no matter how desirable from an economic point of view.

In any event, the current systems are by and large insolvent because of the aging of the population. So either social security taxes are increased exorbitantly, or else government debt could, according to some projections, reach 150 percent of national income in the European Union at large by 2050 and 250 percent in Germany and France. Recall that the debt target ceiling in the Stability and Growth Pact is only 60 percent.

In this chapter, we develop an analytical model in which a pay-as-you-go, old-age security system is designed as a political-economy equilibrium. We then investigate how the aging of the population can shift the equilibrium toward scaling down this fiscal system (thereby encouraging the emergence of individual retirement accounts). We further examine how lifting the ceiling on fiscal deficits can politically facilitate such a scaling down of pay-as-you-go systems and whether such a constitutional reform could come about through the political process.

4.3   A Political-Economy Design for Social Security

In our standard overlapping-generations model, each generation lives for two periods—a working period and a retirement period. We assume a stylized economy in which there are two types of workers—skilled workers who have high productivity and provide one efficiency unit of labor per unit of labor time and unskilled workers who provide only $q < 1$ efficiency units of labor per unit of labor time. Workers have one unit of labor time during their first period of life but are born without skills and thus with low productivity. Each worker chooses whether to acquire an education and become a skilled worker or else to remain unskilled. After the working period, individuals retire, with their consumption funded by private savings and social security pensions (discussed below). There is a continuum of individuals who are characterized by an innate ability parameter e, which is the time needed to acquire an education.

The transfer b is now paid only to the retirees (see below), so that the cutoff level of the education-cost parameter is given by

$$(1 - \tau)w(1 - e^*) - \gamma = (1 - \tau)qw,$$

which yields the same formula as before:

$$e^* = 1 - q - \frac{\gamma}{(1 - \tau)w}. \tag{4.1}$$

To obtain analytical results, we continue to employ a specification in which factor prices are exogenously determined. Thus, we assume a linear production function in which output Y is produced using labor L and capital K—

$$Y = wL + (1 + r)K \tag{4.2}$$

—with capital fully depreciating at the end of the production process.

As before, the population grows at a rate of n. Each individual's labor supply is assumed to be fixed, so that the income tax does not distort individual labor-supply decisions at the margin. But the total labor supply does again depend on the income-tax rate, as this affects the cut-off ability e^* and thus the mix of skilled and unskilled individuals in the economy. At present, the total labor supply is given by

$$L = \left\{ \int_0^{e^*} (1 - e)\, dG + q[1 - G(e^*)] \right\} N_0(1 + n) \equiv \ell(e^*) N_0(1 + n), \tag{4.3}$$

where $N_o(1 + n)$ is the size of the working-age population at present (N_o is the number of young individuals born in the preceding period), and $\ell(e^*) = \int_0^{e^*} (1 - e)\,dG + q[1 - G(e^*)]$ is the average (per-worker) labor supply at present. As before, G is the cumulative distribution function of e, with $G(0) = 0$ and $G(1) = 1$.

There is a pay-as-you-go, old-age social security system by which the taxes collected from the young (working) population are earmarked to finance a pension benefit to the old (retired) population. Thus, the benefit b that is paid to each individual at present must satisfy the following pay-as-you-go budget constraint:

$$bN_0 = \tau wL = \tau w\ell(e^*)N_o(1 + n),$$

where τ is the social security tax at present. Dividing through by N_o yields an explicit formula for the pension benefit:

$$b = \tau wl(e^*)(1 + n). \tag{4.4}$$

In each period, the benefit of the social security system accrues only to the old, whereas the burden (the social security taxes) are borne by the young. One may wonder why the young, who outnumber the old with a growing population, would not drive the tax and the benefit down to zero in a political-economy equilibrium. We appeal to a sort of an implicit intergenerational social contract that goes like this:[4] "I, the young, pay now for the pension benefits of the old, and you, the young of the next generation, will pay for my pension benefit when I grow old and retire." With such a contract in place, the young at present are willing to politically support a social security tax τ that is earmarked to pay the current old-age pension benefit of b because they expect the young generation in the next period to honor the implicit social contract and pay them a benefit αb. The parameter α is assumed to depend negatively on the share of the old in the population. If the current young will each continue to bring n children, then the share of the old will not change in the next period, and α is expected to be one. But if fertility falls, the share of the old in the next period will rise relative to the present, and α is expected to fall below one.

Because factor prices are constant over time, current saving decisions will not affect the rate of return on capital that the current young will earn on their savings. Hence, the dynamics in this model are redundant. For any social security tax rate τ, equations (4.1) and (4.2) determine the functions $e^* = e^*(\tau)$ and $b = b(\tau)$. Denote by $W(e, \tau, \alpha)$ the lifetime income of a young e individual:

$$W(e, \tau, \alpha) = \begin{cases} (1 - \tau)w(1 - e) - \gamma + \alpha b(\tau)/(1+r) & \text{for } e \leq e^*(\tau) \\ (1 - \tau)wq + \alpha b(\tau)/(1+r) & \text{for } e \geq e^*(\tau). \end{cases}$$

(4.5)

In each period, the political-economy equilibrium for the social security tax τ (and the associated pension benefit b) is determined by majority voting among the young and old individuals who are alive in this period. The objective of the old is quite clear: so long as raising the social security tax rate τ generates more revenues and a higher pension benefit b, they will vote for it. However, voting of the young is less clear-cut. Because a young individual pays a tax bill of $\tau w(1 - e)$ or τwq, depending on her skill level, and receives a benefit of $\alpha b/(1+r)$, in present-value terms she must weigh her tax bill against her benefit. She votes for raising the tax rate if $\partial W/\partial \tau > 0$ and for lowering it if $\partial W/\partial \tau < 0$. Note that

$$\partial^2 W(e, \tau, \alpha)/\partial e \partial \tau = \begin{cases} w & \text{for } e < e^*(\tau) \\ 0 & \text{for } e > e^*(\tau). \end{cases}$$

(4.6)

As before, if $\partial W/\partial \tau > 0$ for some e_o, then $\partial W/\partial \tau > 0$ for all $e > e_o$; and similarly, if $\partial W/\partial \tau < 0$ for some e_o, then $\partial W/\partial \tau < 0$ for all $e < e_o$. This implies that if an increase in the social security tax rate benefits a particular young (working) individual (because the increased pension benefit outweighs the increase in the tax bill), then all young individuals who are less able than she is (that is, those who have a higher cost-of-education parameter e) must also gain from this tax increase. Similarly, if a social security tax increase hurts a certain young individual (because the increased pension benefit does not fully compensate for the tax hike), then it must also hurt all young individuals who are more able than she is.

As was already pointed out, the old always opt for a higher social security tax. But as long as $n > 0$, the old are outnumbered by the young. To reach an equilibrium, the bottom end of the skill distribution of the young population joins forces with the old to form a protax coalition of 50 percent of the population, whereas the top end of the skill distribution of the young population forms a counter antitax coalition of equal size. The pivot in determining the outcome of majority voting is a young individual with an education-cost index denoted by e_M, such that the young who have an education-cost index below e_M (namely, the antitax coalition) form 50 percent of the total population. The political-economy-equilibrium tax rate maximizes the lifetime income of this median voter.

Formally, e_M is defined as follows. At present, $N_o(1 + n)G(e_M)$ young individuals have a cost-of-education parameter $e \leq e_M$ (more able than the median voter), and $N_o(1 + n)[1 - G(e_M)]$ young individuals have a cost-of-education parameter $e \geq e_M$ (less able than the median voter). There are also N_o retired individuals at present who always join the protax coalition. Hence, e_M is defined implicitly by

$$N_0(1 + n)G(e_M) = N_o(1 + n)[1 - G(e_m)] + N_o.$$

Dividing this equation by N_o and rearranging terms yield the cost-of-education parameter for the median voter,

$$e_M = G^{-1}\left[\frac{2 + n}{2(1 + n)}\right]. \tag{4.7}$$

As before, the political-equilibrium tax rate τ, denoted by $\tau_o(e_M, \alpha)$, maximizes the lifetime income of the median voter:

$$\tau_0(e_M, \alpha) = \arg \max_{\tau} W(e_M, \tau, \alpha). \tag{4.8}$$

This equilibrium tax rate is implicitly defined by the first-order condition

$$\frac{\partial W[e_M, \tau_0(e_M, \alpha), \alpha]}{\partial \tau} \equiv B[e_M, \tau_0(e_M, \alpha), \alpha] = 0, \tag{4.9}$$

and the second-order condition is

$$\frac{\partial^2 W[e_M, \tau_0(e_M, \alpha), \alpha]}{\partial \tau^2} \equiv B_\tau[e_M, \tau_0(e_M, \alpha), \alpha] \leqq 0, \tag{4.10}$$

where B_τ is the partial derivative of B with respect to its second argument.

4.4   Social Security under Strain: Aging Population

The aging population puts the pay-as-you-go, old-age social security systems under strain. Because the burden of financing the pension benefits to the old falls on fewer young shoulders as a population ages, if the fertility of the current young falls below the fertility rate n of their parents, then the share of the old in the next period will rise and α will fall.

To find the effect of aging on social security, we investigate the effect of a decline in α on the equilibrium social security tax rate $\tau_0(e_M, \alpha)$. Differentiate equation (4.9) totally with respect to α to conclude that

$$\frac{\partial \tau_0(e_M, \alpha)}{\partial \alpha} = -\frac{B_\alpha[e_M, \tau_0(e_M, \alpha), \alpha]}{B_\tau[e_M, \tau_0(e_M, \alpha), \alpha]}, \tag{4.11}$$

where B_α is the partial derivative of B with respect to its third argument. Because $-B_\tau$ is nonnegative [see the second-order condition (4.10)], it follows that the sign of $\partial \tau_0 / \partial \alpha$ is the same as the sign of B_α. It also follows from equation (4.9) that $B_\alpha = \partial^2 W / \partial \alpha \partial \tau$. Employing equation (4.5) we find that

$$B_\alpha[e_M, \tau_o(e_M, \alpha), \alpha] = \frac{\partial^2 W[e_M, \tau_o(e_M, \alpha), \alpha]}{\partial\alpha\partial\tau} = \frac{1}{1+r}\frac{db[\tau_o(e_M, \alpha)]}{d\tau}. \quad (4.12)$$

Naturally, no one will vote for raising the social security tax if $db/dt < 0$ because in such a case, the pension benefit falls when the social security tax is raised. Put differently, a political-economy equilibrium will never be located on the "wrong" side of the Laffer curve, where a tax-rate hike lowers revenue. This can also be seen formally. From equation (4.5),

$$B(e, \tau, \alpha) = \frac{\partial W(e, \tau, \alpha)}{\partial\tau} = \begin{cases} -w(1-e) + \dfrac{\alpha}{1+r}\dfrac{db(\tau)}{d\tau} & \text{for } e \leqq e^*(\tau) \\[2ex] -wq + \dfrac{\alpha}{1+r}\dfrac{db(\tau)}{d\tau} & \text{for } e \geqq e^*(\tau), \end{cases}$$

$$(4.13)$$

so that when the lifetime income of the median voter is maximized—that is, when $B = 0$ [see equation (4.9)]—we have

$$\frac{db[\tau_o(e_M, \alpha)]}{d\tau} = \begin{cases} w(1-e_M)(1+r)/\alpha & \text{if } e_M \leqq e^*(\tau) \\ wq(1+r)/\alpha & \text{if } e_M \geqq e^*(\tau) \end{cases} \geqq 0. \quad (4.14)$$

Thus, it follows from equations (4.12) and (4.14) that $B_\alpha[e_M, \tau_o(e_M, \alpha), \alpha] \geq 0$ and hence from equation (4.11) that

$$\frac{\partial\tau_o(e_M, \alpha)}{\partial\alpha} > 0. \quad (4.15)$$

We conclude that when the young population expects reduced social security benefits because of the aging of the population (that is, when α falls), the public indeed votes for scaling down the social security system at present (that is, for lowering τ and b). As a result, the young resort to supplemental old-age savings, such as individual retirement accounts. The old are worse off as a result of reducing b. But they are outvoted by the young, whose attitude for lowering τ has turned stronger, following the reduction in the social security benefits that they will get.

4.5   Relaxing the Ceiling on Fiscal Deficits

The old continue to oppose the (partial) transition from a pay-as-you-go, old-age social security system to individual retirement accounts because they lose some of their pension benefits. They also have a strong moral claim that they contributed their fair share to the social security system when they were young but receive at retirement less than what they contributed to the social security system at their young age. Their opposition, strengthened perhaps by being morally justified, can be accommodated, in part or in full, if the government is allowed to make a *debt-financed transfer* to the social security system to allow the system to pay pension benefits in excess of the social security tax revenues. This deficit is carried forward to the future, and its debt service is smoothed over the next few generations so that its future tax implications for the current young generation are not significant. This, of course, requires relaxation of some restrictions of the sorts imposed by the Stability and Growth Pact in the European Union during the transition from social security to individual retirement accounts.

For simplicity, suppose that the government makes a transfer of the exact amount that is required to keep the pension benefits of the current old intact, despite the reduction in the social security tax rate. Specifically, when τ falls, then the term b in equation (4.4), which is financed by this τ, falls as well. But we assume that the government compensates the old generation to maintain total pension benefits intact. Therefore, despite the fall in b, the old are indifferent to the reduction in τ (and consequently to the reduction in b). Thus, the outcome of the majority voting is now effectively determined by the young only. The median voter is now a median among the young population only. This median voter has a lower cost-of-education index than before—that is, e_M will fall.

To find the effect of the fall in e_M on the political-economy-equilibrium social security tax rate $\tau_0(e_M, \alpha)$, we follow the same procedure as in the preceding section and conclude that

$$\frac{\partial \tau_0}{\partial e_M} = -\frac{B_{e_M}[e_M, \tau_0(e_M, \alpha), \alpha]}{B_{\tau}[e_M, \tau_0(e_M, \alpha), \alpha]}. \tag{4.16}$$

As before, the sign of $\partial \tau / \partial e_M$ is the same as the sign of B_{e_M} because $B_\tau \leq 0$. Note that $B_{e_M} = \partial^2 W / \partial e_M \partial \tau$ [see equation (4.9)], so that it follows from equation (4.5) that

$$B_{e_M}[e_M, \tau_0(e_M, \alpha), \alpha] = \begin{cases} w & \text{for } e_M < e^*(\tau) \\ 0 & \text{for } e_M > e^*(\tau). \end{cases} \tag{4.17}$$

Thus, we conclude that $\partial \tau / \partial e_M$ is nonnegative: it is positive when the median voter is a skilled individual (that is, when $e_M < e^*$) and zero when the median voter is an unskilled individual (that is, when $e_M > e^*$). Hence, a decline in e_M decreases (or leaves intact) the social security tax $\tau_0(e_M, \alpha)$ and the associated benefit b.

The rationale for this result is straightforward. All unskilled people have the same lifetime income, regardless of their cost-of-education parameter e. Therefore, the attitude toward the (τ, b) pair is the same for all of them. Hence, the change in the median voter has no affect on majority voting when this median voter is an unskilled individual. For skilled individuals, lifetime income increases when the education-cost parameter e declines. Because the social security system is progressive with respect to the cost-of-education parameter, the net benefit from it (i.e., the present value of the expected pension benefit minus the social security tax) declines, as lifetime income increases (i.e., as e falls). Thus, a decline in the cost-of-education parameter of the median voter e_M lowers the political-economy-equilibrium social security tax and pension benefit.

Thus, making the fiscal constraints of the sorts imposed by the Stability and Growth Pact in the European Union more flexible may facilitate the political-economy transition from a national pay-as-you-go, old-age social security system to a fully funded private pension system. Such a transition improves the viability of the national system but at a cost of a lesser degree of redistribution (which is an inherent feature of a national system).[5]

4.6   Conclusion

The idea of the European Union's Stability and Growth Pact is to prevent governments from running loose fiscal policies at the expense of other euro-based countries. This spillover effect could happen through higher interest rates if the European Central Bank offset the fiscal laxity with tight monetary policy or through higher risk premium on euro-based government bonds. But the Pact, as it is rigidly constructed, neglects long-term fiscal considerations and creates political-economy impediments to social security reforms that if implemented can improve the fiscal balance in the future. The EU's highest court ruled on July 12, 2004, that finance ministers acted illegally in suspending the threat of sanctions against France and Germany over their repeated breach of the EU's budget deficit rules. The ruling gave new urgency to the debate in Europe about how to reform the Stability and Growth Pact.

An aging population shakes the public finances of pay-as-you-go, old-age social security systems, and in a political-economy framework these deteriorated balances lead to the downsizing of the social system and the emergence of supplemental individual retirement accounts. Indeed, the existence of a negative correlation between the dependency ratio (which increases with the aging of the population) and labor-tax rates is demonstrated in chapter 2 in a 1970s through 1990s sample that includes twelve Western European countries and the United States. Similarly, a negative correlation is found between the dependency ratio and per-capita social transfers (of which old-age social security captures the lion's share). These findings are consistent with the hypothesis of this chapter that aging populations put political-economic pressure on governments to downsize pay-as-you-go, old-age national systems.

5   The Capital-Tax-Financed Welfare State

5.1 Introduction

In the preceding chapter, we develop the hypothesis that contemporary phenomena such as aging and low-skill migration generate political processes that must eventually downscale the welfare state.[1] Our model welfare state is financed primarily by labor-income taxes, as is typically the case in reality. In this chapter, we turn to examine whether capital-income taxation, as an alternative to labor-income taxation, can come to the rescue of the welfare state.

In every life-cycle saving framework (for instance, the overlapping-generations model), the burden of a tax on capital income falls most heavily on the shoulders of the elderly, whose income is primarily derived from capital. The current young become capital-income taxpayers only later, when they grow older and accumulate savings. A change in the age composition of the population therefore has potentially strong implications for the political economy of capital-income taxation.

In this chapter, we first develop a simple model of a political-economy determination of capital-income taxation in the framework of overlapping generations. The capital-income tax revenues now replace (or add to) the previous labor-tax revenues in financing a uniform lump-sum transfer (demogrant), so that the combined tax-transfer system is progressive, as in the modern welfare state.

Conventional wisdom suggests that a rising share of the elderly in the population should tilt the political-power balance against taxes on capital income because the old are the primary owners of capital. This hypothesis is first examined theoretically in the present chapter. In chapter 6, we confront the theoretical conclusions with data from the ten Western European countries over the period 1970 through 1996. We show that the implications of the model are largely consistent with the data.

5.2   Exogenous Capital-Income Tax

The heart of any political-economy equilibrium must be some underlying distribution of income. For concreteness, our model generates, as before, an income distribution based on a human-capital-formation framework, with an exogenously given heterogenity in innate ability. We continue to work with a standard overlapping-generations model in which each generation lives two periods—a working period and a retirement period. However, we focus now on capital-income taxation, where the labor-income tax is exogenously determined. For simplicity, we set the labor-tax rate equal to zero.

Evidently, a capital-income tax distorts saving and consumption decisions. To abstract from the distortion associated with human-capital investment, we assume for simplicity that $\gamma = 0$. In this case, the cut-off level e^*—such that individuals with an education-cost parameter below e^* will invest in education and become skilled, whereas everyone else remains unskilled—is given by

$$w(1 - e^*) = qw,$$

and rearranging terms yields

$$e^* = 1 - q. \tag{5.1}$$

Thus, essentially, the cut-off level e^* is exogenous—that is, it is not distorted by the tax.

Suppose that the government levies a flat capital-income tax denoted by τ to finance a uniform transfer denoted by b. It is assumed that the tax revenues in each period are used fully to finance the transfer in the same period—essentially, a pay-as-you-go system. Because an individual is born with no capital, only the old have any capital income in each period. On the other hand, the young, who own no capital yet, constitute a majority of the population as long as the population-growth rate n is positive. Thus, in any majority-voting system the young majority will attempt to institute a 100 percent tax on the income from capital (held only by the old minority) and, if feasible, will even confiscate the capital principal in addition to the income generated from it. To eliminate such an implausible outcome from the model, we assume that any capital-income-tax change must last for at least two periods and that this provision is deemed credible. In this case, the young will realize that raising the capital-income-tax rate will increase their tax burden as well because the tax hike applies to their capital income in the next period when they grow old.

The tax rate and the generosity of the grant are linked through the government's budget constraint. In a multiperiod setting, this simple specification captures the spirit of a pay-as-you-go, tax-benefit (transfer) system.

We continue to assume a small open economy with free capital mobility. In this case, the domestic interest rate r must be equal to the (assumed fixed) world rate of interest. With a constant-returns-to-scale production technology, this means that the wage rate per efficiency unit of labor w is fixed too. We assume also that the residence principle of taxation is adopted by our small open economy.[2] That is, income of residents is taxed irrespective of its origin, whether at home or abroad; income of nonresidents is fully exempted from tax. This means that the capital-income-tax base is equal to the interest from domestic savings because only these savings are taxed, whether they are invested domestically or abroad.

In the current period t, the savings of the old are already pre-determined, so that the capital-income-tax base is also given. Thus, there is no efficiency cost to taxing the income from these savings. As noted, the government's budget is balanced period by period. Thus, the transfer (b_t^A) that is paid to both the young (the workers) and the old (the retirees) in period t (the first period of the two-period political cycle) is given by

$$b_t^A N_0 [(1+n)^{t-1} + (1+n)^t] = \tau r s_{t-1}^A N_0 (1+n)^{t-1},$$

where s_{t-1}^A is the average saving of the old in period t (which was predetermined in period $t-1$). Rearranging terms yields

$$b_t^A = \frac{\tau r s_{t-1}^A}{2+n}. \tag{5.2}$$

We emphasize that s_{t-1}^A is exogenously given in period t, since it is determined by the choices made by the now old in the previous period.

Similarly, the transfer (b_{t+1}^B) paid in period $t+1$ (the second period of the two-period cycle) is given by

$$b_{t+1}^B = \frac{\tau r s_t^B}{2+n}, \tag{5.3}$$

but now s_t^B is the *average* (over the young population) saving made by the young in period t—that is,

$$s_t^B = \int_0^1 s_t^B(e)\, dG, \tag{5.4}$$

where $s_t^B(e)$ is the saving made by a young individual with an education-cost parameter e. Unlike s_{t-1}^A, s_t^B is not given in period t; it will be determined by utility-maximizing young individuals in period t. It is thus endogenously determined by the tax (τ) and transfer (b_t^A, b_{t+1}^B) parameters.

We denote by $W(e, \tau, b_t^A, b_{t+1}^B)$ the lifetime income (wealth) of a young individual with an ability parameter e who is born in period t:

$$W(e, \tau, b_t^A, b_{t+1}^B) = \begin{cases} w(1-e) + b_t^A + \dfrac{b_{t+1}^B}{1+(1-\tau)r} & \text{for } e \leqq e^* \\[4mm] wq + b_t^A + \dfrac{b_{t+1}^B}{1+(1-\tau)r} & \text{for } e \geqq e^*. \end{cases} \tag{5.5}$$

Note that due to the capital-income tax, the discount rate is the net-of-tax interest rate—that is, $(1-\tau)r$.

A standard utility function $u(c_{1t}, c_{2t})$ is maximized over first-period consumption (c_{1t}) and second-period consumption (c_{2t}), subject to the lifetime budget constraint

$$c_{1t} + \frac{c_{2t}}{1+(1-\tau)r} = W(e, \tau, b_t^A, b_{t+1}^B). \tag{5.6}$$

The maximized value of u, known as the *indirect-utility function*, is a function of the lifetime income and the net-of-tax discount factor and is denoted by

$$V\{W(e, \tau, b_t^A, b_{t+1}^B), [1+(1-\tau)r]^{-1}\}. \tag{5.7}$$

The saving of a young individual in period t—$S\{W(e, \tau, b_t^A, b_{t+1}^B), [1+(1-\tau)r]^{-1}\}$—equals the present value of second-period consumption

$$S(\cdot) = C_2(\cdot)[1+(1-\tau)r]^{-1}, \tag{5.8}$$

where $C_2(\cdot)$ is the demand function of second-period consumption. Substituting equation (5.4) into equation (5.3) yields

$$b_{t+1}^B = \frac{\tau r}{2+n} \int_0^1 S\{W(e, \tau, b_t^A, b_{t+1}^B), [1+(1-\tau)r]^{-1}\} \, dG. \tag{5.9}$$

As can be seen from equation (5.5), all individuals with an ability parameter e above e^* (the unskilled individuals) have the same wealth and consequently the same saving (and utility). Using equation (5.5), we can therefore rewrite equation (5.9) as follows:

$$b^B = \frac{\tau r}{2+n} \int_0^{e^*} S\{w(1-e) + b^A + b^B[1 + (1-\tau)r]^{-1},$$

$$[1 + (1-\tau)r]^{-1}\} dG + \frac{\tau r}{2+n} S\{wq + b^A + b^B[1 + (1-\tau)r]^{-1},$$

$$[1 + (1-\tau)r]^{-1}\}[1 - G(e^*)]. \tag{5.10}$$

Because w and r are fixed, the economy reaches the steady-state cycle at once. We therefore drop the time subscripts t and $t+1$ in equation (5.10) and henceforth. Note also that there is a proportion of $1 - G(e^*)$ of unskilled individual among the working-age population.

Given the capital-income-tax rate τ, we now have a complete description of the equilibrium. Equation (5.2) determines b^A as a function of τ and n (note that s^A is exogenous and thus is independent of τ), whereas equation (5.10) determines b^B as a function of the same variables:

$$b^A = B^A(\tau, n) \tag{5.2'}$$

$$b^B = B^B(\tau, n). \tag{5.10'}$$

5.3   Endogenous Capital-Income Tax

We now return to describe how the capital-income tax is determined in a political-economy setting. As before, we assume that the political process takes place in a direct democracy. That is, people vote directly for the tax rate, taking into account the budget-balancing benefits b^A and b^B as determined in equations (5.2') and (5.10'), respectively.

Consider first an old individual with an ability parameter e. Her saving, denoted by $s^A(e)$, has already been predetermined. Note that s^A in equation (5.2) or (5.2') is the average of the saving of the old. Her net gain from the tax-transfer system (denoted by β) is given by

$$\beta(\tau, n, e) = B^A(\tau, n) - \tau r s^A(e). \tag{5.11}$$

Note that $s^A(e)$ is strictly declining in e for all $e \leqq e^*$ (assuming, of course, normality) and then becomes flat. Thus, if a certain tax hike benefits an old person with ability parameter e_0, it must also benefit all old people with an ability parameter above e_0 (that is, all less able individuals). Conversely, if an e_0 person favors a certain tax cut, then all persons with a lower e (the more able) will also favor such a tax cut. To see this formally, note from equation (5.11) that $\partial(\partial\beta/\partial\tau)/\partial e = \partial^2\beta/\partial\tau\partial e = -r\,ds^A/de \leq 0$.

Consider next a young individual of type e. Expressing the transfers b^A and b^B as functions of τ and n, as in equations (5.2') and (5.10'), respectively, we can rewrite her indirect utility function as

$$\hat{V}(\tau, n, e)$$

$$= \begin{cases} V\{w(1-e) + B^A(\tau, n) + B^B(\tau, n)[1 + (1-\tau)r]^{-1}, [1 + (1-\tau)r]^{-1}\} \\ \qquad \text{for } e \leqq e^* \\ V\{wq + B^A(\tau, n) + B^B(\tau, n)[1 + (1-\tau)r]^{-1}, [1 + (1-\tau)r]^{-1}\} \\ \qquad \text{for } e \geqq e^*. \end{cases} \tag{5.12}$$

As with the old, we can calculate how the net gain from a tax change varies with e:

$$\frac{\partial^2 \hat{V}}{\partial\tau\partial e}(\tau, n, e)$$

$$= \begin{cases} -w_1\left(V_{11}(\cdot)\left\{\dfrac{\partial B^A}{\partial\tau}(\cdot) + \dfrac{\partial B^B}{\partial\tau}(\cdot)[1 + (1-\tau)r]^{-1}\right. \\ \left.\left. + rB^B(\cdot)[1 + (1-\tau)r]^{-2}\right\} + rV_{12}(\cdot)[1 + (1-\tau)r]^{-2}\right) & \text{for } e < e^* \\ 0 & \text{for } e > e^*, \end{cases}$$
$$\tag{5.13}$$

where subscripts stand for partial derivatives. At this point, we plausibly assume that $\partial^2 \hat{V} / \partial \tau \partial e \geq 0$. For instance, with a log-linear utility function, $V_{11} < 0$; $V_{12} = 0$; and because raising the tax rate must raise revenue at the equilibrium range of tax rates (that is, $\partial W / \partial \tau = \partial B^A / \partial \tau + \partial B^B / \partial \tau [1 + (1 - \tau)r]^{-1} + rB^B[1 + (1 - \tau)r]^{-2} > 0)$, it follows that $\partial^2 \hat{V} / \partial \tau \partial e$ is indeed nonnegative. In this case, if a certain tax hike benefits a young individual of type e_1, it must benefit all individuals with $e > e_1$. Conversely, if a tax cut is beneficial for an e_1 individual, it must also be beneficial for all individuals with $e < e_1$.

A political-economy equilibrium can be now specified compactly. There is a triplet (τ^*, e_O, e_Y) such that

$$\tau^* = \underset{\tau}{\operatorname{argmax}} \ \beta(\tau, n, e_O), \tag{5.14}$$

$$\tau^* = \underset{\tau}{\operatorname{argmax}} \ \hat{V}(\tau, n, e_Y), \tag{5.15}$$

and

$$G(e_O) + G(e_Y)(1 + n) = (2 + n)/2. \tag{5.16}$$

This implies that there are two individuals—one old (with an ability parameter e_O) and one young (with an ability parameter e_Y)— who each plays the role of a "pivot" for her respective generation. Note that these pivots' preferred choice in equilibrium is the same tax rate τ^* [see equations (5.14) and (5.15)]. Together, these pivots divide the total population (of the old and the young) evenly, so that the preferred tax rate τ^* is consistent with the outcome of democratic voting. All old individuals with ability parameters above e_O and all young individuals with ability parameters above e_Y would prefer a higher tax rate than (or, at least, the same tax rate as) τ^*. All old individuals with ability parameters below e_O and all young individuals with ability parameters below e_Y would prefer a lower tax rate than (or the same tax rate as) τ^*. To see that these pivots divide the total population (of the old and the young) evenly, note that the number of old people with ability parameters below e_O is $G(e_O)N_0(1+n)^{t-1}$. Similarly, the number of young individuals with ability parameters below e_Y is $G(e_Y)N_0(1+n)^t$. The rest of the population (who favor a higher tax rate than τ^*) is $[(1 - G(e_O)] \cdot N_0(1+n)^{t-1} + [1 - G(e_Y)]N_0(1+n)^t$. Equating the latter expression with $G(e_O)N_0(1+n)^{t-1} + G(e_Y)N_0(1+n)^t$ yields equation (5.16).

Given the structure of the model, the determination of the political-economy equilibrium can be simplified a great deal. To see this, differentiate β with respect to τ to get

$$\frac{d\beta}{d\tau}(\tau, n, e) = \frac{\partial B^A}{\partial \tau}(\tau, n) - rs^A(e) = \frac{rs^A}{2+n} - rs^A(e), \tag{5.17}$$

where use is made of equation (5.2). Note that this derivative is independent of τ so that each individual gains from raising the tax all the way to 100 percent (when this derivative is positive for her), gains from lowering it all the way down to zero (when this derivative is negative for her), or is indifferent to the tax (when this derivative is zero for her). Recall that s^A is the average (over the old population only) saving of the old, whereas $s^A(e)$ is the saving of just an old individual of type e. Because $s^A(e)$ is declining in e, the ability parameter of the old pivot is determined by

$$\frac{s^A}{2+n} = s^A(e_O). \tag{5.18}$$

This e_O depends on the population-growth rate, n; denote it by $E_O(n)$. All old individuals with an ability parameter above $E_O(n)$—and hence individual saving $s^A(e)$ below the total saving of the old per the total population $s^A/(2+n)$—would (weakly) benefit from a tax hike up to a maximum of 100 percent, whereas all the rest would (weakly) benefit from a tax cut all the way down to zero. The pivot among the old, however, is indifferent to any level of the tax rate and therefore will not play an effective role in setting the tax rate. Note that it may be possible that $s^A/(2+n) < s^A(e)$ for all e, in which case the old pivot is $E_O(n) = 1$. In this case, all old individuals object to any tax on capital income.[3]

Thus the equilibrium condition in equation (5.14) becomes redundant as the old pivot is determined by (5.18), and she is indifferent among all tax rates. Substituting $E_O(n)$ into equation (5.16) determines the ability parameter of the young pivot; denote this by $e_Y = E_Y(n)$. The political-economy-equilibrium tax rate is then finally derived by substituting $E_Y(n)$ for e_Y into equation (5.12) and setting the derivative of $\hat{V}$ with respect to τ equal to zero. That is, the political-economy equilibrium is effectively determined by the young pivot according to

$$\hat{V}_1[\tau, n, E_Y(n)] = 0. \tag{5.19}$$

The solution to this equation constitutes the political-economy-equilibrium tax rate, denoted by $\tau^*(n)$.

5.4   Aging and Capital-Income Taxation

In a life-cycle saving framework such as the overlapping-generations model employed here, a tax on capital applies immediately to the current old, whose income is derived primarily from capital. Only one period later, when the current young grow older, do they bear the capital-tax burden as well. Therefore, at any point in time, the antitax coalition would be expected to draw heavily on the current old generation. Thus, as the population ages and the share of the elderly in the population rises, the antitax coalition also would be expected to increase its influence and the ensuing political-economy equilibrium to involve lower taxes on capital.

We turn to address this issue. In our setting, the share of the elderly in the population is $No(1+n)^{t-1}/[No(1+n)^{t-1} + No(1+n)^t]$ $= 1/(2+n)$. Thus, when the population-growth rate (n) falls, the share of the elderly in the population rises. We therefore focus on the question of whether $d\tau^*/dn$ is indeed positive, so that when n declines (and the share of the elderly in the population rises), the political-economy capital-income-tax rate falls.

For this purpose we totally differentiate equation (5.19), the single equation that effectively determines the political-economy-equilibrium tax rate on capital income, with respect to n to get

$$\frac{d\tau^*}{dn} = \frac{\hat{V}_{12} + \hat{V}_{13}\,dE_Y/dn}{-\hat{V}_{11}}. \tag{5.20}$$

As previously, subscripts denote partial derivatives, and the arguments of the functions were dropped for ease of notation. Because τ^* maximizes $\hat{V}$, it follows, as before, from the second-order condition for maximization that $\hat{V}_{11} \leq 0$, so that

$$\text{Sign}\left(\frac{d\tau^*}{dn}\right) = \text{Sign}(\hat{V}_{12} + \hat{V}_{13}\,dE_Y/dn). \tag{5.21}$$

Thus, the effect of n on τ^* is decomposed into two components. First, $\hat{V}_{12}$ represents the effect of a change in n on the preferred tax by the existing young pivot. Second, a change in n changes the identity of the young pivot and, correspondingly, the equilibrium tax rate; this is represented by $\hat{V}_{13}\,dE_Y/dn$. (As has been mentioned, the old pivot does not play an active role in the determination of the tax rate.)

We are now well equipped to address the question of whether a rise in the elderly share in the population (namely, a decline in n) does indeed lower the capital-income-tax rate in a political-economy equilibrium. Formally put, is $d\tau^*/dn$ indeed positive? We show, however, contrary to the aforementioned common wisdom, that the latter derivative may plausibly be negative rather than positive.

To see this, we first investigate the sign of $\hat{V}_{12}$, which represents the attitude toward the capital-income tax of the existing young pivot. Note from equation (5.12) that

$$\hat{V}_1 = V_1 \frac{\partial W}{\partial \tau} + V_2 \frac{\partial R}{\partial \tau}, \tag{5.22}$$

where R is the discount factor—that is, $R = [1 + (1 - \tau)r]^{-1}$.

The net gain to the young pivot from raising the tax rate consists of two components—an income effect [the first term on the right-hand side of equation (5.22)] and a price (interest-rate) effect [the second term on the right-hand side of equation (5.22)] that is related to the efficiency cost of taxation. To see how the incentive to raise the tax (that is, $\hat{V}_1$, which is zero at the existing n) changes when n rises, differentiate the expression in (5.22) with respect to n to get

$$\hat{V}_{12} = \frac{\partial}{\partial n} \left(V_1 \frac{\partial W}{\partial \tau} \right) + \frac{\partial}{\partial n} \left(V_2 \frac{\partial R}{\partial \tau} \right). \tag{5.23}$$

The first term on the right-hand side of equation (5.23) is plausibly negative on two mutually enforcing grounds. First, when n rises, taxes collected from the old in the current period are shared (via the transfer b^A) by more young people, thereby reducing the transfer b^A to everyone, including the young pivot, who is decisive. This reduces the net gain to the young pivot from raising the tax rate. Second, when n rises, the taxes collected in the second period, when the current young become old, are now shared by more newly born young individuals. Therefore, the transfer b^B that the current young pivot will receive in the second period of her life, when she turns old, is also reduced. Put differently, when n rises and the share of the elderly in the population declines, the first term on the right-hand side of equation (5.23) may be negative because of a "fiscal leakage" from the young pivot to others (namely, the other current-period young and all of the next-period young). The second term on the right-hand side of equation (5.23) has to do with how an increase in n changes the price (and efficiency cost) component of $\hat{V}_1$, the net gain to the young pivot from raising the tax on capital. We cannot, however, a priori sign this term. If the distortion is small, this term is also small. Nevertheless, because of the first term (the "fiscal-leakage" effect), $\hat{V}_{12}$ may be negative, so that the net gain to the existing young from raising the tax diminishes.

To complete the analysis of the sign of $d\tau^*/dn$, we must also examine the sign of $\hat{V}_{13}\, dE_Y/dn$, which represents the effect of a change in the identify of the young pivot on the equilibrium tax rate. This term tends to be rather small and may even altogether vanish. For instance, it does indeed vanish when the young pivot is an unskilled individual because $\hat{V}_{13} = 0$ in this case [see equation (5.13)]. That is, the new pivot and the existing young pivot, being both unskilled, have identical attitudes toward taxation.

To sum up, we have demonstrated how $d\tau^*/dn$ may plausibly be negative. That is, as the population ages and the share of the elderly in the population rises (namely, as n declines), the capital-income-tax rate and the transfers in the political-economy equilibrium may plausibly rise. The main driving force for this result is the fiscal-leakage effect.

5.5 Conclusion

Aging may boost the size of the welfare state when capital-income taxation is employed to finance the benefits provided by the welfare state. Aging has an opposite effect on the size of the welfare state when the benefits granted by it are financed by labor taxes (as is demonstrated in chapters 2 and 4). Can capital-income taxation indeed rescue a welfare state with an aging population, as may be concluded from this chapter? We cannot give a positive answer at this stage because we do not know yet whether capital tax can generate sufficient revenue in a globalized world economy. In the next part of the book, we examine whether strong international tax competition in the era of globalization imposes severe constraints on capital-income taxation and thereby put into question its standing in the public finance of the welfare state.

6

Aging and the Welfare State: Empirical Evidence

6.1 Introduction

Our model may suggest opposing effects of aging on labor taxation and capital taxation. We may conclude that aging generates political processes that downscale the welfare state when the benefits that it provides are financed by labor taxes. These processes may upscale the welfare state when the benefits are financed through capital-income taxes. In this chapter, we provide integrative empirical evidence of the effects of aging on labor, capital taxes, and benefits provided by the welfare state. We examine whether patterns in the data for ten European countries over the period 1970 through 1996 are consistent with the predictions of the theory regarding the relationship between the aging of the population and the tax rate on labor income, capital income, and social transfers.[1] Capital-tax rates are set in conjunction with taxes on labor income, the largest source of revenue in the advanced economies. We present results for specifications in which the regression equations for the capital-tax rate are estimated jointly with those for labor taxes, allowing for an interaction between the two. Among other things, we use the predictions of our theories on the implications of aging for the political-economy equilibrium concerning different sources of public finances to identify the two tax rates. As noted in the preceding chapters, the capital-income tax depends on the balance of interests between the old and the young, whereas the equilibrium for labor-income tax depends on the balance between working individuals and dependents: these are overlapping but not identical populations. In addition, we make use of the notion that capital crosses borders relatively more easily than labor, so that capital-tax rates in open economies are more likely to be subject to international tax competition than is the case for labor-tax rates (see an extensive analysis in part 2).

Control variables for capital-tax rates can be thought of as comprising several groups. First, we include two measures of exposure to the international flows of capital to take into account the impact of capital mobility on governments' setting of tax rates through international tax competition. These measures are the ratio of the stock of international portfolio investment to GDP and the ratio of the stock of international direct investment to GDP. Both are measured as the total stock of international investment and not as the flow in a single year. By *gross stock*, we mean the sum of inflows and outflows in absolute value. This set of variables captures a country's overall integration with international capital, both inward and outward investment, though domestic capital can be potentially (but not necessarily in realization) mobile and thus affected by international tax competition in ways not captured by our data.

The next set of variables is meant to control for factors that affect the size of the welfare state—both government's need for revenue and residents' demands for social services. The control variables are the share of government employment out of total employment (to indicate the breadth of government involvement in the economy) and a measure of openness to trade (to capture exposure to external real-sector shocks). As before, openness is included to address the hypothesis made by Rodrik (1998) that an important function of the welfare state is to provide social insurance against the adverse effects of external shocks. Thus, large governments would be expected to be found in open economies. Alternately, Alberto Alesina and Romain Wacziarg (1998) suggest that the empirical connection between openness and the size of government comes about indirectly through a size effect. Small countries are both more open than large countries and have larger government spending as a share of national income (and thus higher taxes than large economies). We further include a measure of income inequality—the ratio of the income share of the top quintile to the combined share of the middle three quintiles ("rich versus middle"). As has been pointed out, this variable—denoted as the *skewness-of-income distribution*— is suggested by previous political-economy theories that seek to explain the size of the welfare state (e.g., Meltzer and Richard, 1981; Persson and Tabellini, 2003). Finally, as before, to control for business-cycle effects that might affect revenue requirements, we also include the real GDP growth.

The specification for the labor-tax-rate regressions is as in chapter 2. The explanatory variables include the total dependency ratio (or the old dependency ratio), openness to trade flows, the share of government jobs in total employment, GDP growth, and the income-distribution variable.

6.2   Data: Sources and Description

Data on capital- and labor-tax rates are based on Mendoza, Razin, and Tesar (1994) (as extended by Mendoza, Milesi-Ferretti, and Asea, 1997) and Daveri and Tabellini (2000). The effective average rates of taxation are derived by using revenue statistics. A brief description of how these tax rates are calculated appears in the appendix to this chapter. Data on the share of the old in the population are from the World Development Indicators (World Bank, various years). Regressions use the share of those age sixty-four and older out of the total population, though the results are not affected by taking the share of the old out of only the population of individuals fourteen years and older, which might correspond to the working-age population.

Data on the stock (not flows) of international capital investment are from Philip Lane and Gian Maria Milesi-Ferretti (2001). These are the estimated stock of inward and outward direct-investment assets (adjusted for relative stock-market price variations) and the stock of portfolio equity assets and liabilities (adjusted for stock-market price variations).

The OECD Analytical Database (2003) is used to calculate measures of per-capita GDP, government employment as a share of total employment, and openness to trade (defined as the sum of the imports plus exports as a share of GDP). The total dependency ratio is defined as one minus the labor force as a share of the population (rather than as the number of dependents per working individual). The measures of income skewness are derived from the updated inequality database of Deininger and Squire (1996), which provides measures of income shares by quintile over time, though data are not available for every year. Only the high-quality measures in the database are used, and the missing observations are then obtained through linear interpolation (these shares do not vary all that much over time, though in most countries there is a general trend toward increased inequality).

As shown in table 6.1, the data encompass slightly different periods for the countries, so that an unbalanced panel is used in the regressions. Tax rates on capital income vary across countries, from a low of under 14 percent in Spain to over 50 percent in Sweden and the United Kingdom (the latter having the lowest tax rate on labor income on average over the sample period). The importance of international investment varies substantially across countries, with a great deal of inward and outward investment in the Netherlands and United Kingdom and relatively little in others. This is even more true of portfolio investment, though the data end for many countries before important steps forward in European

Table 6.1
Summary Statistics (169 observations)

Country	Age	Old per Population	Labor Tax	Capital Tax	Government Job Share	Dependents per Population	Trade Openness	FDI/GDP	International Portfolio Stock per GDP	GDP Growth
Spain	80–86	11.5	32.6	13.8	11.1	63.5	39.7	8.6	0.9	1.7
Austria	70–92	14.8	37.4	21.1	17.7	56.1	69.7	6.6	1.8	3.0
France	82–96	14.0	46.5	26.2	23.2	56.2	44.4	17.5	7.9	1.9
Germany	70–96	14.9	39.1	27.5	14.6	54.0	50.1	9.6	5.2	2.7
Netherlands	85–92	12.6	52.0	30.5	13.7	60.4	103.2	65.7	32.7	2.8
Belgium	70–91	14.2	42.6	34.7	18.0	59.6	121.8	19.6	3.5	2.7
Norway	81–91	15.8	39.2	40.5	26.5	50.0	74.5	13.3	2.3	2.4
Finland	86–92	13.2	34.0	45.3	21.1	48.8	49.8	10.8	0.6	0.8
Sweden	71–92	16.5	46.5	52.0	29.7	48.6	59.6	13.8	1.9	1.7
United Kingdom	70–96	14.9	25.7	56.5	19.7	52.2	52.1	41.1	23.1	2.1

capital-market integration were taken in 1992 following the single-market act.

6.3 Estimation Results

Table 6.2 provides results from a set of regressions for the determinants of the capital- and labor-tax rates. All specifications include a complete set of country fixed effects (not shown in the tables). The regressions thus take into account the fact that richer countries tend

Table 6.2
Determinants of Capital- and Labor-Tax Rates (169 observations)

	OLS		2SLS		3SLS	
	Capital	Labor	Capital	Labor	Capital	Labor
Old per population	2.033		3.532		2.820	
	(2.23)		(2.58)		(2.27)	
Dependency ratio		−0.438		−0.443		−0.443
		(−3.59)		(−3.43)		(−3.61)
Capital-tax rate				−0.054		0.030
				(−0.68)		(0.41)
Labor-tax rate			2.493		2.295	
			(1.60)		(1.63)	
Foreign direct-investment stock	0.199		0.001		0.116	
	(1.90)		(0.00)		(0.77)	
Portfolio stock	−0.335		−0.418		−0.440	
	(−3.84)		(−3.83)		(−4.41)	
Trade openness	−0.026	0.117	−0.285	0.113	−0.282	0.113
	(−0.38)	(5.19)	(−1.60)	(4.63)	(−1.74)	(4.87)
Government job share	0.876	0.827	−1.805	0.907	−1.512	0.907
	(3.26)	(10.94)	(−1.06)	(6.36)	(−0.98)	(6.68)
GDP growth	−0.711	−0.073	−0.603	−0.116	−0.594	−0.116
	(−4.18)	(−1.25)	(−3.04)	(−1.31)	(−3.25)	(−1.38)
Income skewness	−0.152	0.077	−0.313	0.069	−0.309	0.070
	(−3.04)	(4.12)	(−2.73)	(3.64)	(−2.95)	(3.82)
R^2	0.432	0.204	0.178	0.241	0.897	0.960

Note: All specifications include country fixed effects (coefficients not shown). OLS is ordinary least squares. 2SLS and 3SLS are two- and three-stage least squares.

to have higher tax rates and provide more generous welfare benefits than poor countries do.

The first two columns show single-equation results estimated by
using ordinary least squares (OLS) (this is a panel fixed-effect specification). We then provide results in which the two taxes depend on
one another—first estimating regressions for each variable sepa-
rately using two-stage least squares (2SLS) and then with the two
estimated jointly by three-stage least squares (3SLS). Both estimators allow for the endogeneity of the two tax rates with respect to
each other, with the latter estimates further allowing for common
shocks to both regressions. We now discuss the estimates for each
technique in turn, focusing first on the equations for the influences
of the capital-tax rates.

The coefficient of the share of the old in the population is positive and statistically significant in the capital-tax equations, with all
three estimation techniques. The results indicate that the tax rate on
capital income goes up by two to three percentage points for each
one percentage point increase in the share of the old in the population. This seemingly counterintuitive result is quite consistent with
the implication of the theory. The old are less than a majority of
voters in all countries in our sample, so that the young will naturally want to levy taxes on capital and thus shift the burden of taxation to older individuals who tend to be owners of capital. Further,
the young will be more inclined to do so when there are more old
people to pay the capital-income tax and fewer young people to
share the tax revenues that finance the transfers. The coefficient
becomes larger in magnitude with the system estimates, but the
results are qualitatively the same.

The coefficients on the other explanatory variables in the capital-
tax-rate regression likewise provide sensible results with all three
estimation techniques. We discuss the coefficient of the openness
variables in detail in chapter 8.

The coefficient of the share of government workers out of total
employment has a significant positive effect in the OLS regression

but a negative, though not statistically significant, coefficient in the two-stage least-squares and three-stage least-squares results. The difference arises from labor taxes, which are included in the latter two equations. Because the government-jobs variable has a strongly positive coefficient in the labor-tax equations, this variable by itself in the ordinary-least-squares capital-tax regressions appears to be picking up some of the effect of the omitted labor-tax variable.

The coefficients on GDP growth and income distribution are again consistent across the three estimators. Stronger growth is associated with lower tax rates—a feature shared with labor taxes as well. This is likely due to the larger tax base with lower tax rates. In addition, there may be at play a reverse-causality effect from the tax rates to growth: lower tax rates (and fewer distortions) may promote growth. A distribution of income more skewed to the richest quintile is associated with a statistically significant lower tax rate on capital but with a higher tax rate on labor. This is a somewhat puzzling result. One possibility for it is that it stems from a different lobbying intensity on the part of the two groups, something that we do not capture in our model.

The labor-tax rate has a positive coefficient in the latter two capital-tax regressions, though this is significant at only the 10 percent confidence level. While not conclusive, this suggests that the capital-tax rate is effectively set as a complement to the labor tax rather than as a substitute (in addition to the other influences). In contrast, the coefficient of the capital-tax rate is far from statistically significant in the two specifications where this variable appears as an influence on the labor tax.

The results for the influences of the tax rate on labor income are in line with previous evidence provided in chapter 2 (despite a slight difference in the sample of countries, owing to data limitations on the capital-tax rates and international capital stocks). This is the case in both the single-equation and system estimators. The dependency ratio has a statistically negative coefficient. As noted above, this negative association is along the lines of the relationship between the capital tax and the share of the old in the population. Remember that dependent individuals are a minority of voters, so the majority of working individuals naturally favors lower taxes and transfers as the number of dependents rises. Openness to goods-trade flows is associated with a statistically significant higher tax rate, in accordance with the theory of Rodrick (1998) or the interpretation of Alesina and Wacziarg (1998), whereas more unequal income distribution leads to higher labor tax rates, as in Meltzer and Richards (1981).

6.4   Conclusion

The empirical results for the relationship between capital-tax rates, labor-tax rates, and the aging of the population (or the increase in the share of dependents in the population) are thus in close alignment with the predictions of political-economy theory. The capital-income tax rises and the labor tax falls when the share of the old in the population rises (due to a fiscal-leakage effect). We also find that globalization may have opposing effects on labor and capital taxation. Greater trade openness raises the labor-tax rates (and social transfers) but has an insignificant effect on capital-tax rates. On the other hand, greater capital openness (as measured by the stock of foreign portfolio investments) has a statistically significant depressing effect on capital taxation. A possible explanation for the negative effect of capital openness on capital taxes is international tax competition, which is discussed in part 2.

6.5   Appendix: Capital- and Labor-Tax Rates

6.5.1   Labor Taxes

The effective tax rate on labor income is defined as the percentage difference between post- and pretax labor income. In practice, however, computing this tax rate is difficult because of the manner in which data on income taxes and other taxes based on labor income are reported. One common problem that also affects most calculations of aggregate labor-income-tax rates is that tax-revenue sources typically do not provide a breakdown of individual income-tax revenue in terms of labor and capital income. This is due to the fact that tax returns are generally filed to cover all of a taxpayer's income, regardless of its origin. This problem is addressed by assuming that all sources of the households' income are taxed at the same rate—an assumption that according to 1991 statutory-tax rates in OECD member countries is a good approximation (OECD, 1991). Another issue of concern is the fact that, in addition to the individual income tax on wages, there are other important taxes on labor income (such as social security contributions and payroll taxes) that need to be taken into account (Barro and Sahasakul, 1986).

First, the households' average tax rate on total income (τ_H) is defined as

$$\tau_H = \left(\frac{1100}{OSPUE + PEI + W}\right), \tag{6.1}$$

where from the OECD revenue statistics 1100 is taxes on income, profits, and capital gains of individuals and from the National Accounts $OSPUE$ is the operating surplus of private unincorporated enterprises, PEI is households' property and enterpreneurial income, and W is wages and salaries.

Then the effective tax rate on labor income (τ_L) is defined by

$$\tau_L = \frac{\tau_H W + 2000 + 3000}{W + 2200}, \tag{6.2}$$

where 2000 is total contribution to social security, 2200 is employers' contribution to social security, and 3000 is taxes on payroll and workforce.

6.5.2 *Capital Taxes*

Similarly, the effective tax rate on capital income (τ_K) is defined by

$$\tau_K = \frac{\tau_H(OSPUE + PEI) + 1200 + 4100 + 4400}{OS},$$

where 1200 is taxes on income, profits, and capital gains of individuals, 4100 is recurrent taxes on immovable property, 4400 is taxes on financial and capital transactions, and OS is total operating surplus of the economy.

II   Globalization

7

Capital Taxation: The Shadow of International Tax Competition

7.1 Introduction

As is shown in part 1 of this book, aging generates political forces that tend to curtail the size of the welfare state when the social transfers that it provides are financed by labor taxes. Aging also may generate political forces that tend to boost a capital-tax-financed welfare state. Part 1 asks whether a capital tax can indeed replace a labor tax and thereby rescue the aging welfare state. In part 2, we analyze how capital-market globalization exerts downward pressure on the size of the welfare state through international tax competition. Therefore, in the end, the downsizing of an aging welfare state is unavoidable.

In this chapter, we present a simple analytical framework for the study of capital taxation in the presence of international capital mobility. In particular, we analyze the tax structure in the political-economy equilibrium.

7.2 International Capital Mobility: A Stylized Political-Economy Tax Model

We present a stripped-down model of international capital mobility that enables us to explore key issues of international taxation without being sidetracked by irrelevant complications. This is an extension of the model described in chapter 2. We consider an economy that lives for two periods, indexed by $t = 1, 2$. There is one aggregate, all-purpose good in each period that serves for both consumption and investment.

7.2.1 Consumers

As in chapter 2, there are two types of workers: skilled workers have high productivity and provide one efficiency unit of labor per unit of labor time, and unskilled workers provide $q < 1$ efficiency units of labor per unit of time. Workers have one unit of labor time during each one of the two periods of their life. They are born without skills and thus with low productivity. In the first period, each worker chooses whether to get an education and become a skilled worker or instead to remain unskilled.

There is a continuum of individuals that is characterized by an innate-ability parameter e, which is the time needed to acquire a skill. By investing e units of labor time in education in the first period, a worker becomes skilled, after which the remaining $(1 - e)$ units of labor time in the first period provide an equal amount of efficiency units of labor in the balance of the first period. We now assume that the individual also provides one efficiency unit of labor in the second period. We assume a positive pecuniary cost of acquiring skills γ, which is not tax-deductible.

Given these assumptions, there exists, again, a cutoff level e^*, such that those with education-cost parameters below e^* will invest in education and become skilled, whereas everyone else remains unskilled. The cutoff level is determined by the equality between the present value of the payoff to education and the cost of education (including forgone income):

$$(1 - \tau_L)(1 - q)\left[w_1 + \frac{w_2}{1 + (1 - \tau_D)r}\right] = (1 - \tau_L)w_1 e^* + \gamma, \qquad (7.1)$$

where w_t is the wage rate per efficiency unit of labor in period $t = 1, 2$; r is the domestic rate of interest; τ_L is the tax rate on labor income (constant over time); and τ_D is the tax rate on capital income of residents from domestic sources (see below). Note that unlike the model in part 1, we now have both taxes on labor and capital at the same time. Rearranging terms, equation (7.1) yields

$$e^* = (1 - q)\left[1 + \frac{w_2/w_1}{1 + (1 - \tau_D)r}\right] - \frac{\gamma}{(1 - \tau_L)w_1}. \tag{7.2}$$

Note that the two taxes—the tax on labor income and the tax on capital income—have opposite effects on the decision to acquire skill. The tax on labor income reduces the forgone (net-of-tax) income component of the cost of education. It also reduces the payoff to education by the same proportion.[1] Were the pecuniary cost γ equal to zero (or else tax-deductible), the labor-income tax would have no effect on the decision to acquire skill. However, with a positive pecuniary cost of education, the labor-income tax has a negative effect on acquiring skills: it reduces e^* and, consequently, also the proportion of the population who becomes skilled [namely, $G(e^*)$]. On the other hand, the tax on capital income has a positive effect on education because it reduces the (net-of-tax) discount rate, thereby raising the present value of the future payoff to education.

We continue to assume for the sake of simplicity that the individual's leisure time is exogenously given. Nevertheless, total labor supply is distorted by the taxes, as can be seen from equation (7.2). Note that there are $G(e^*)$ skilled individuals and $1 - G(e^*)$ unskilled individuals in each period. The labor supply of each one of the unskilled individuals, in efficiency units, is q in each period. Therefore, total labor supply in efficiency units of the unskilled individuals is $q[1 - G(e^*)]$ in each period. However, a skilled individual devotes e units of her time in the first period to acquire education and hence works only $1 - e$ units of time in the first period. Thus, the individual labor supply in the first period varies over e.

The labor supply of skilled individuals is equal to $\int_0^{e^*} (1-e)\,dG$. Any skilled individual supplies as labor all of her unit time in the second period. Thus, total labor supply (L_t) in efficiency units in period $t = 1, 2$, is given by

$$L_1 = \int_0^{e^*} (1-e)\,dG + q[1 - G(e^*)] \tag{7.3}$$

and

$$L_2 = G(e^*) + q[1 - G(e^*)]. \tag{7.4}$$

For the sake of simplicity, assume that all individuals have identical preferences over first- and second-period consumption [$c_1(e)$ and $c_2(e)$, respectively], represented by a common, concave utility function $u[c_1(e), c_2(e)]$.[2] Each individual has initial income (endowment) in the first period of I_1 units of the consumption-capital good. The total amount of the initial endowment (I_1 because the size of the population is normalized to one) serves as the stock of capital employed in the first period. (This initial endowment is generated by past savings or is inherited.) Because taxation of the fixed initial endowment is not distortionary, we may assume that the government could efficiently tax away the entire value of the initial endowments. Thus, an individual of type e faces the following budget constraints in periods 1 and 2, respectively:

$$c_1(e) + s_D(e) + s_F(e) = E_1(e) + T_1, \tag{7.5}$$

and

$$c_2(e) = T_2 + E_2(e) + s_D(e)[1 + (1 - \tau_D)r]$$
$$+ s_F(e)[1 + (1 - \tau_F - \tau_N^*)r^*], \tag{7.6}$$

where $E_t(e)$ is after-tax labor income, net of the cost of education $t = 1, 2$, and where T_t is a uniform lump-sum transfer (demogrant) in period $t = 1, 2$. That is,

$$E_1(e) = \begin{cases} (1 - \tau_L)(1 - e)w_1 - \gamma & \text{for } e \leq e^* \\ (1 - \tau_L)qw_1 & \text{for } e \geq e^*, \end{cases} \tag{7.7}$$

and

$$E_2(e) = \begin{cases} (1 - \tau_L)w_2 & \text{for } e \leq e^* \\ (1 - \tau_L)qw_2 & \text{for } e \geq e^*. \end{cases} \tag{7.8}$$

An individual can channel savings to either the domestic or foreign capital market because the economy is open to international capital flows. We denote by $s_D(e)$ and $s_F(e)$ savings channeled by an e individual to the domestic and foreign capital market, respectively. We denote by r and r^* the real rate of return in these markets, respectively.[3] The government levies a tax at the rate τ_D on capital (interest) income from domestic sources. Capital (interest) income from foreign sources is subject to a nonresident tax at the rate of τ_N^*, levied by the foreign government. The domestic government may levy an additional tax on its domestic residents on their foreign-source income at an effective rate of τ_F. Note that $\tau_F + \tau_N^*$ is the effective tax rate on foreign-source income of residents.

For the sake of brevity, we consider only the case of a capital-exporting country (that is, its national savings exceed domestic investment) with the difference (defined as the current account surplus) invested abroad.[4] (The analogous case of a capital-importing country can be worked out similarly.) By arbitrage possibilities, the net-of-tax rates of interest, earned at home and abroad, are equalized—that is,

$$(1 - \tau_D)r = (1 - \tau_F - \tau_N^*)r^*. \tag{7.9}$$

Employing (7.9), one can consolidate the two one-period budget constraints (7.5) and (7.6) into one lifetime budget constraint:

$$c_1(e) + Rc_2(e) = E_1(e) + RE_2(e) + T, \tag{7.10}$$

where

$$R = [1 + (1 - \tau_D)r]^{-1} \tag{7.11}$$

is the net-of-tax discount factor (which is also the relative after-tax price of second-price consumption) and

$$T \equiv T_1 + RT_2 \tag{7.12}$$

is the discounted sum of the two transfers (T_1 and T_2).[5]

As usual, the consumer maximizes her utility function, subject to her lifetime budget constraint. A familiar first-order condition for this optimization is that the intertemporal marginal rate of substitution is equated to the tax-adjusted interest factor:

$$MRS(e) \equiv u_1[c_1(e), c_2(e)] / u_2[c_1(e), c_2(e)]$$

$$= 1 + (1 - \tau_D)r = R^{-1}, \tag{7.13}$$

where u_i denotes the partial derivative of u with respect to its ith argument, $i = 1, 2$. Equations (7.13) and (7.10) yield the consumption-demand functions $\bar{c}_1[R, E_1(e) + RE_2(e) + T]$ and $\bar{c}_2[R, E_1(c) + RE_2(e) + T]$ of an e individual. The maximized value of the utility function of an e individual, $v[R, E_1(e) + RE_2(e) + T]$, is the familiar indirect-utility function.

Denote the aggregate consumption demand in period $t = 1, 2$ by

$$C_t[R, (1 - \tau_L)w_1, (1 - \tau_L)w_2, T]$$

$$\equiv \int_0^1 \bar{c}_t[R, E_1(e) + RE_2(e) + T] \, dG$$

$$= \int_0^{e^*} \bar{c}_t[R, (1 - \tau_L)(1 - e)w_1 + R(1 - \tau_L)w_2 + T - \gamma] \, dG$$

$$+ [1 - G(e^*)]\bar{c}_t[R, (1 - \tau_L)qw_1 + R(1 - \tau_L)qw_2 + T], \tag{7.14}$$

where use is made of equations (7.7) and (7.8). Note that e^* is a function of $(1 - \tau_L)w_1$ and of Rw_2/w_1 [see equation (7.2)].

7.2.2 Producers

All firms are identical and possess constant-returns-to-scale technologies, so that with no further loss of generality we assume that there is only one firm, which behaves competitively. Its objective, dictated by the firm's shareholders, is to maximize the discounted sum of the cash flows accruing to the firm. We assume that the firm finances its investment by issuing debt. In the first period, it has a cash flow of $(1 - \tau_D)[F(K_1, L_1) - w_1 L_1] - [K_2 - (1 - \delta)K_1] + \tau_D \delta K_1$, where $F(\cdot)$ is a neoclassical, constant-returns-to-scale production function. In the second period, the firm has an operating cash flow of $(1 - \tau_D)[F(K_2, L_2) - w_L L_2] + (1 - \delta)K_2 + \tau_D \delta K_2$. We denote by δ both the physical and economic rates of depreciation (assumed for the sake of simplicity to be equal to each other). This depreciation rate is also assumed to apply for tax purposes. We essentially assume that the corporate income tax is fully integrated into the individual income tax. With such integration of the individual income tax and the corporate tax, there is no difference between debt and equity finance. Specifically, we assume that the individual is assessed a tax (at the rate τ_D) on the profits of the firm, whether or not they are distributed, and that there is no tax at the firm level. The firm's discounted sum of its after-tax cash flow is therefore

$$\pi = (1 - \tau_D)[F(K_1, L_1) - w_1 L_1] - [K_2 - (1 - \delta)K_1] + \tau_D \delta K_1$$
$$+ \{(1 - \tau_D)[F(K_2, L_2) - w_2 L_2]$$
$$+ \tau_D \delta K_2 + (1 - \delta)K_2\}/[1 + (1 - \tau_D)r]. \tag{7.15}$$

Note that K_1 is the preexisting stock of capital at the firm, carried over from period zero. Maximizing (7.15) with respect to K_2, L_1, and L_2 yields the standard marginal-productivity conditions:

$$F_L(K_1, L_1) = w_1, \tag{7.16}$$

$$F_L(K_2, L_2) = w_2, \tag{7.17}$$

and

$$F_K(K_2, L_2) - \delta = r. \tag{7.18}$$

Note that although taxes do not affect the investment rule of the firm, nevertheless, the taxes are distortionary. To see this distortion, consider the intertemporal *marginal rate of transformation* (MRT) of second-period consumption (namely, c_2) for first-period consumption (namely, c_1). It is equal to $(1 - \delta) + F_K(K_2, L_2)$: when the economy gives up one unit of first-period consumption to invest it, then it receives in the second period the depreciated value of this unit (namely, $1 - \delta$) plus the marginal product of capital (namely, F_K). From equation (7.18), we can see that

$$MRT = 1 + r.$$

However, from equation (7.13) we can see that the common intertemporal marginal rate of substitution of all individuals is equal to

$$MRS = 1 + (1 - \tau_D)r.$$

Hence, the MRT need not equal the MRS. In fact, the MRT is larger than the MRS when the tax rate on capital income from domestic sources (τ_D) is positive. This violates one of the Pareto-efficiency conditions.

Note that the firm has pure profits (or surpluses) stemming from the preexisting stock of capital K_1. We denote this surplus by π_1, which is equal to

$$\pi_1 = (1 - \tau_D)[F(K_1, L_1) - \delta K_1 - w_1 L_1] + K_1. \tag{7.19}$$

The surplus consists of the after-tax profit of the first period, plus the level of the preexisting stock of capital. Given the constant-returns-to-scale technology, the firm's after-tax cash flow consists entirely of this surplus—that is, $\pi = \pi_1$. This equality follows by substituting the Euler's equation, $F(K_2, L_2) = F_K(K_2, L_2)K_2 +$

$F_L(K_2, L_2)L_2$, and the marginal-productivity conditions, equations (7.17) and (7.18), into equation (7.15). Naturally, the government fully taxes away the surplus π_1 before resorting to distortionary taxation (via the various $\tau's$).

7.2.3   Policy Tools: Taxes, Transfers, and Debt

The government has a consumption demand of C_t^G in period $t = 1, 2$. We assume that the government can lend or borrow at market rates. With no loss of generality, we assume that the government operates only in the foreign-capital market—that is, its first-period budget surplus is invested abroad. For concreteness, suppose that this is positive. Therefore, the government has to balance its budget not period by period but only over the two-period horizon:

$$C_1^G + R^*C_2^G + T_1 + R^*T_2 = \tau_L w_1 L_1 + \tau_L R^* w_2 L_2 + \tau_D R^* r S_D$$
$$+ \tau_F R^* r^* S_F + \pi_1 + \tau_D [F(K_1, L_1) - \delta K_1$$
$$- w_1 L_1], \tag{7.20}$$

where

$$S_D = \int_0^1 s_D(e)\, dG \tag{7.21}$$

is the aggregate private savings, channeled into the domestic capital market;

$$S_F = \int_0^1 s_F(e)\, dG \tag{7.22}$$

is the foreign aggregate private savings, channeled into the foreign-capital market; and

$$R^* = [1 + (1 - \tau_N^*)r^*]^{-1} \tag{7.23}$$

is the foreign discount rate faced by the domestic economy. Note that the foreign government levies a tax at the rate τ_N^* on interest income from the home government budget surplus invested abroad.

The left-hand side of equation (7.20) represents the present value of the government expenditures on public consumption and transfers, discounted by the factor R^*, which is the interest factor at which the domestic economy can lend. The right-hand side of equation (7.20) represents the present value of the revenues from the labor-income taxes, the interest-income taxes, and the pure surplus of the firm.

Market clearance in the first period requires that

$$CA + C_1 + C_1^G + K_2 - (1 - \delta)K_1 + G(e^*)\gamma = F(K_1, L_1), \tag{7.24}$$

where CA is the current account surplus.[6] Market clearance in the second period requires that

$$C_2 + C_2^G = F(K_2, L_2) + (1 - \delta)K_2 + CA[1 + (1 - \tau_N^*)r^*]. \tag{7.25}$$

Note that the tax at the rate τ_N^* is levied by the foreign country on the interest income of the residents of the home country and must therefore be subtracted from the resources available to the home country.

To get one present-value resource constraint, we can substitute the current account surplus CA from equation (7.24) into equation (7.25):

$$C_1 + R^*C_2 + C_1^G + R^*C_2^G + K_2 - (1 - \delta)K_1 + G(e^*)\gamma$$

$$= F(K_1, L_1) + R^*F(K_2, L_2) + R^*(1 - \delta)K_2. \tag{7.26}$$

Note that we may ignore the government budget constraint (7.20) by Walras's law because constraint (7.20) will be satisfied when equation (7.26) (the economywide "budget" constraint) and equation (7.10) (the individual budget constraints) both hold. This is demonstrated in the appendix to this chapter.

7.2.4 Political-Economy Tax-Transfer Equilibrium

As before, the median voter can be shown to be the decisive voter. Therefore, the political-economy-equilibrium tax rates maximize the (indirect) utility of the median voter. Denoting the indirect-utility function of the median voter by V,

$$V(e_M, R, w_1^N, w_2^N, T) = \begin{cases} v[R, (1 - e_M)w_1^N + Rw_2^N + T - \gamma] & \text{if } e_M < e^* \\ v[R, q(w_1^N + Rw_2^N) + T] & \text{if } e_M > e^*, \end{cases}$$

where $w_t^N = (1 - \tau_L)w_t$ is the after-tax wage per efficiency unit of labor in period $t = 1, 2$.

Policy tools at the government's disposal include labor-income taxes and capital-income taxes. We therefore assume that the government can effectively choose the after-tax wage rates (w_1^N and w_2^N) and the after-tax discount factor (R). The government can choose also T, the discounted sum of the lump-sum transfers (T_1 and T_2). Once w_1^N, w_2^N, R, and T are chosen, then private-consumption demands $[C_1(R, w_1^N, w_2^N, T)$ and $C_2(R, w_1^N, w_2^N, T)]$ are determined. The cutoff level e^* and labor supplies L_1 and L_2 are also determined as follows:

$$e^*(R, w_1^N, w_2^N) = (1 - q)[1 + Rw_2^N/w_1^N] - \gamma/w_1^N, \tag{7.2$'$}$$

$$L_1(R, w_1^N, w_2^N) = \int_0^{e^*(R, w_1^N, w_2^N)} (1 - e)\, dG + q\{1 - G[e^*(q, w_1^N, w_2^N)]\}, \tag{7.3$'$}$$

and

$$L_2(R, w_1^N, w_2^N) = G[e^*(R, w_1^N, w_2^N)] + q\{1 - G[e^*(R, w_1^N, w_2^N)]\}. \tag{7.4$'$}$$

In choosing its policy tools (R, w_1^N, w_2^N, and T) and its public-consumption demands (C_1^G and C_2^G), the government is constrained by the economywide "budget" constraint (7.26), where C_1, C_2, L_1, L_2, and e^* are replaced by the functions $C_1(\cdot), C_2(\cdot), L_1(\cdot), L_2(\cdot)$, and

$e^*(\,\cdot\,)$, given by equations (7.14) and (7.2′) through (7.4′), respectively. Note that the capital stock in the first period (K_1) is exogenously given. The capital stock in the second period (K_2) must satisfy the investment rule of the firm [equation (7.18)]. Note that because the economy is financially open, the individuals, by the arbitrage condition [equation (7.9)], are indifferent between chaneling their savings domestically or abroad. This means that the government can choose K_2, and then r and the pretax wages (w_1 and w_2) are determined to clear the capital market and labor market in each period through equations (7.18), (7.16), and (7.17), respectively. This does not mean that the government actually chooses the stock of capital (K_2) for the firm, the pretax wage rates (w_1 and w_2), or the domestic interest rate (r). Rather, w_1, w_2, and r are determined by market clearance, and the firm chooses K_2 to maximize its value. What we did is to determine K_2, w_1, w_2, and r at levels that are compatible with firm-value maximization and market clearance in the presence of taxes.

To sum up, the government in a political-economy equilibrium chooses $C_1^G, C_2^G, R, w_1^N, w_2^N, T$, and K_2 to maximize the utility of the median voter [as given by equation (7.27)], subject to the economy-wide "budget" constraint, equation (7.26). Note that C_1, C_2, L_1, L_2, and e^* in the latter constraint are replaced by the functions $C_1(\,\cdot\,), C_2(\,\cdot\,), L_1(\,\cdot\,), L_2(\,\cdot\,)$, and $e^*(\,\cdot\,)$, respectively.

Note that in this maximization, K_2 appears only in the economy-wide "budget" constraint, equation (7.26). Thus, the first-order condition for the political-economy equilibrium level of K_2 is given by

$$1 - R^* F_K(K_2, L_2) - R^*(1 - \delta) = 0. \tag{7.28}$$

Note that this choice does not depend on whether the median voter is skilled or unskilled.

Substituting the firm's investment rule, equation (7.18), and rearranging terms yield

$$1 - \delta + F_K(K_2, L_2) = 1 + (1 - \tau_N^*)r^*. \tag{7.29}$$

The political-economy-equilibrium stock of capital [implicitly determined from equation (7.29)] conforms with Peter A. Diamond and James A. Mirrlees's (1971) aggregate-production-efficiency theorem: the intertemporal marginal rate of transformation [which is $1 - \delta + F_K(K_2, L_2)$] must be equated to the world intertemporal marginal rate of transformation faced by the domestic economy [which is equal to $1 + (1 - \tau_N^*)r^*$].

This rule can be seen in figure 7.1, where first-period total (private and public) consumption $(C_1 + C_1^G)$ is plotted on the horizontal axis and second-period total consumption $(C_2 + C_2^G)$ on the vertical axis. Suppose that L_1, L_2, and e^* were already set at their political-economy-equilibrium levels. The production-possibility frontier is described by the curve ABD, whose slope is equal (in absolute value) to $(1 - \delta) + F_K(K_2, L_2)$. The optimal-tax stock of K_2 is HD,

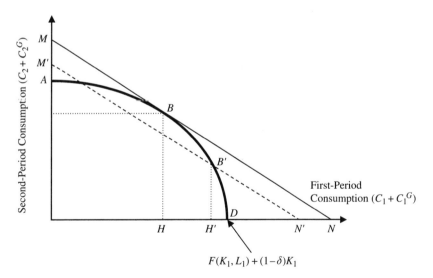

Figure 7.1
The optimal-tax stock of capital (K_2)

which gives rise to the consumption-possibility frontier given by
MBN. Any other level of K_2 (say, $H'D$) must generate a lower
consumption-possibility frontier—the curve $M'B'N'$.

Employing the firm's investment rule [the marginal productivity
condition (7.18)] and the arbitrage condition [equation (7.9)], we can
conclude from equation (7.29) that

$$r = (1 - \tau_N^*)r^*. \tag{7.30}$$

That is, the pretax domestic rate of interest r must be equated to the
world rate of interest faced by the domestic economy, which is the
world rate of interest, net of the source taxes. Equations (7.9) and
(7.30) yield the political-economy-equilibrium tax on foreign-source
income:

$$\tau_F = \tau_D(1 - \tau_N^*). \tag{7.31}$$

Thus, in the political-economy equilibrium, the home country
imposes the same tax rate (τ_D) on foreign-source income from capital as on domestic-source income from capital, except that a deduc-
tion is allowed for foreign taxes paid (and levied at source). One
euro earned abroad is subject to a tax at the source at the rate τ_N^*;
the after-foreign-tax income, which is $1 - \tau_N^*$, is then taxed by the
home country at the rate τ_D. The total effective tax rate paid on
foreign-source income is therefore

$$\tau_F + \tau_N^* = \tau_D + \tau_N^* - \tau_N^*\tau_D.$$

7.3   International Tax Competition and Capital Taxation

A critical issue of taxation in the era of globalization of the capital
markets is the ability of national governments to tax their residents
on foreign-source capital income. A *New York Times* editorial ("A
Retreat on Tax Havens," 2001, p. 9) underscores the severity of this
issue:

From Antigua in the Caribbean to Nauru in the South Pacific, offshore tax havens leach billions of dollars every year in tax revenues from countries around the world.... The Internal Revenue Service estimates that Caribbean tax havens alone drain away at least $70 billion per annum in personal income tax revenue. The OECD suspects the total worldwide to be in the hundreds of billions of dollars.... The most notorious tax havens do not even extend their minimal tax rates to their own citizens or domestic enterprises. Their primary aim is to encourage and profit from individuals and businesses seeking to evade taxes in their own countries.

It is fairly safe to argue that tax havens and the inadequacy of cooperation among national tax authorities in the OECD in information exchanges put binding ceilings on how much foreign-source capital income can be taxed. What, then, are the implications for taxes on domestic-source capital income?

Consider the extreme situation where the home country cannot effectively enforce any tax on the foreign-source capital income of its residents. That is, suppose that $\tau_F = 0$. Then we can see from the political-equilibrium tax rule that applies to foreign-source capital income [equation (7.31)] that the tax rate on domestic-source capital income, τ_D, would be set to zero too. Thus, the capital-income tax vanishes altogether. And even if some enforcement of taxation on foreign-source capital income is feasible so that τ_F does not vanish altogether, it still follows from equation (7.31) that $\tau_D = \tau_F/(1 - \tau_N^*)$, so that a low τ_F generates a low τ_D. Indeed, a poor enforcement of international taxes would generate political processes that curtail any burden of capital-income taxation.

The unwillingness of foreign tax authorities to cooperate with the home tax authority in helping to enforce capital taxation on the capital income of residents of the home country originating abroad usually stems from their desire to lure capital to their countries. This is what is meant by *tax competition*. They further compete with the home country by lowering the source tax (τ_N^*) that they levy on the capital income of the residents of the home country. We thus capture formally the effect of tax competition by assuming that τ_N^*

falls. Then we can see from equation (7.30) that r, the net (of depreciation δ) marginal product of domestic capital, must rise. With diminishing marginal product, this happens when the stock of domestic capital falls and more capital flows abroad. Hence, the tax base for the domestic-source capital income shrinks, thereby turning the enforcement of foreign-source capital income all the more acute. Thus, a welfare state that relies on capital taxes is akin to a house built on sand.

7.4   Conclusion

Our stripped-down general-equilibrium model of a political-economy determination of capital taxation with a free mobility of capital internationally shows how international tax competition severely curtails the scope of capital taxation as a means of finance for welfare-state benefits. Therefore, an aging welfare state, governed by political-economy forces, cannot avoid the tough task of downscaling its size by resorting to capital taxes to finance the social transfers that it provides.

7.5   Appendix: Walras's Law

In this appendix, we demonstrate that the government budget constraint [equation (7.26)] is redundant because it must be satisfied when equations (7.26) and (7.10) hold (Walras's law).

Substituting the definitions of $E_1(e)$ and $E_2(e)$ in equations (7.7) and (7.8), respectively, into the individual budget-constraint [equation (7.10)], aggregating over all individuals and dividing by R yields

$$C_1/R + C_2 = T_1/R + T_2 + (1 - \tau)w_1L_1/R + (1 - \tau_L)w_2L_2$$

$$- G(e^*)\gamma/R, \tag{7.32}$$

where use is made of the definitions of L_1 and L_2 in equations (7.3) and (7.4), respectively. Divide the economywide "budget-constraint" [equation (7.26)] by R^*, and subtract it from equation (7.32) to get

$$C_1\left(\frac{1}{R}-\frac{1}{R^*}\right)-\frac{T_1}{R}-T_2-\frac{(1-\tau_L)w_1L_1}{R}-(1-\tau_L)w_2L_2$$

$$+G(e^*)\gamma\left(\frac{1}{R}-\frac{1}{R^*}\right)-\frac{C_1^G}{R^*}-C_2^G-\frac{K_2-(1-\delta)K_1}{R^*}+\frac{F(K_1,L_1)}{R^*}$$

$$+F(K_2,L_2)+(1-\delta)K_2=0. \tag{7.33}$$

Note that:

$$\frac{1}{R}-\frac{1}{R^*}=1+(1-\tau_D)r-[1+(1-\tau_N^*)r^*]=-\tau_F r^* \tag{7.34}$$

by equation (7.9). Substituting equation (7.34) into equation (7.33) yields

$$-\tau_F r^* C_1 - \frac{T_1}{R^*} + \tau_F r^* T_1 - T_2 - \frac{(1-\tau_L)w_1L_1}{R^*} + \tau_F r^*(1-\tau_L)w_1L_1$$

$$-(1-\tau_L)w_2L_2 - \tau_F r^* G(e^*)\gamma - \frac{C_1^G}{R^*} - C_2^G - \frac{K_2-(1-\delta)K_1}{R^*}$$

$$+\frac{F(K_1,L_1)}{R^*}+F(K_2,L_2)+(1-\delta)K_2=0. \tag{7.35}$$

Substituting the definition of π_1 from equation (7.19) and Euler's equation [namely, $F(K_2,L_2)=F_K(K_2,L_2)K_2+F_L(K_2,L_2)L_2=(r+\delta)K_2+w_2L_2$, by the marginal productivity conditions (7.17) and (7.18)] into equation (7.35) yields

$$\tau_F r^*[T_1+(1-\tau_L)w_1L_1-C_1-G(e^*)\gamma]-\frac{T_1}{R^*}-T_2+\frac{\pi_1}{R^*}+\frac{\tau_L w_1L_1}{R^*}$$

$$+\tau_L w_2L_2+rK_2-\frac{K_2}{R^*}+K_2-\frac{C_1^G}{R^*}-C_2^G$$

$$+\frac{\tau_D[F(K_1,L_1)-\delta K_1-w_1L_1]}{R^*}=0. \tag{7.36}$$

Finally, substituting the arbitrage condition [equation (7.9)] into equation (7.36) and multiplying by R^* yield

$$R^*\tau_F r^*[T_1 + (1 - \tau_L)w_1 L_1 - C_1 - G(e^*)\gamma - K_2] + R^*\tau_D r K_2 + \tau_L w_1 L_1$$

$$+ R^*\tau_L w_2 L_2 + \pi_1 + \tau_D[F(K_1 L_1) - \delta K_1 - w_1 L_1]$$

$$= C_1^G + R^* C_2^G + T_1 + Rq^* T_2. \tag{7.37}$$

Note that the government has effectively appropriated the initial stock of capital K_1 by fully taxing away the surplus stemming from it. Therefore, the households must finance through their savings [which is $T_1 + (1 - \tau_L)w_L L_1 - C_1$] all three forms of investment—the investment in human capital $G(e^*)\gamma$, the entire new domestic stock of domestic capital K_2, and the private financial investment abroad. Consequently,

$$S_D = K_2 \tag{7.38}$$

and

$$S_F = T_1 + (1 - \tau_L)w_1 L_1 - C_1 - G(e^*)\gamma - K_2. \tag{7.39}$$

Substituting equations (7.38) and (7.39) into equation (7.37) yields the consolidated government budget constraint equation (7.20), validating Walras's law.

8 The Downward Convergence of Capital Taxation across Countries: Evidence from the European Union

8.1 Introduction

Our theory suggests that because of international tax competition, capital-market globalization generates political-economy processes that curtail capital taxes. In this chapter, we supplement this finding with some empirical evidence from the European Union (EU).

8.2 Capital Taxes: Panel Data

In chapter 6 (table 6.2), we provide estimates of determinants of capital-tax rates in a sample of ten EU countries over the period 1970 through 1996.[1] Among the determinants are three openness variables that we now elaborate on.

The first variable is the gross stock of international portfolio assets (that is, both the stock that foreigners invested in the country and the stock that residents of this country invested abroad).[2] Its coefficient is negative and significant (at the 1 percent level) in both the ordinary-least-squares (OLS) regression and the two-stage and three-stage least-squares (2SLS and 3SLS) regressions. This result is in line with the notion that there is international tax competition for relatively mobile portfolio investments, so that a country with more mobility has lower capital tax rates. This hypothesis is further supported by James R. Hines (1999), Peter Birch Sorensen (2000), Tim

Besley, Rachel Griffith, and Alexander Klemm (2001), Michael
P. Devereux, Griffith, and Klemm (2002), Devereux and Griffith
(2002), and Lassen and Sorensen (2002).

The second variable is the gross stock of foreign direct-
investment (FDI) assets. However, its coefficient is not statistically
different from zero in the systems equations. The greater "fixity" of
direct investment, compared to portfolio investment, likely lessens
the importance of international tax competition, accounting for this
finding of little effect of direct investment on the setting of capital-
tax rates. Also, foreign direct investments often qualify for a special
tax treatment by the host country, so that the host's effective tax
rate need not be related to the averatge tax rate on capital income.
In addition, FDI stock may generate intrafirm trade, so that it may
be correlated with the measure of trade opennenss (see below).
Therefore, the coefficient turns out to be statistically insignificant.

The aforementioned two variables relate to the globalization of
capital markets. The third variable is trade openness as measured
by the volume of trade (imports plus exports of goods and services). Its coefficient is negative in all three equations but is not
statistically different from zero. This might indicate that countries
that are open along other dimensions (such as goods trade) face
more tax competition on capital and that capital openness and
goods-trade openness are correlated in the sample. We note also
that trade openness has positive and significant effects on the labor-
tax rate in all three regressions. One possible interpretation is that
with the erosion of the base for capital taxation, resorting to labor
taxation is inevitable.[3]

8.3   The Effects of the European Single Market

The creation of a single market in Europe is a rare natural experi-
ment on the effects of capital-market openness on capital-income

taxation. We highlight the effects of this event on the corporate sector in the European Union.

The *statutory* tax rates have indeed declined since the 1970s by from eleven percentage points (Germany) to twenty-six percentage points (Ireland). However, the meaningful tax rates from an economic point of view are the *effective* tax rates, which may subtantially differ from the statutory rates. We therefore calculate effective tax rates on corporate income. These calculations are based on the well-known work of Hall and Jorgenson (1967), who introduced the user-cost-of-capital approach.[4] We follow here the formula for the effective tax rate on corporate income (τ_e) refined by Alan J. Auerbach (1983):[5]

$$\tau_e = \frac{(r+\delta)(1 - \tau_s z) - (r+\delta)(1 - \tau_s)}{(r+\delta)(1 - \tau_s z) - \delta(1 - \tau_s)},$$

where r is the real rate of return that the firm must earn after corporate taxes (by instruction of its shareholders), δ is the physical rate of depreciation (assumed exponential), τ_s is the statutory corporate-tax rate, and z is the present value of depreciation allowances.[6]

The calculations were carried out for fourteen EU countries for the period 1974 through 2000. The countries are Austria, Belgium, Denmark, Finland, France, Germany, Ireland, Italy, Luxembourg, the Netherlands, Portugal, Spain, Sweden, and the United Kingdom. The results are depicted in figure 8.1. One can clearly detect a downward breakpoint at the end of the 1980s in the wake of the single-market event. Overall, the mean EU effective corporate tax rate went down from 42 percent in 1975 to 32 percent in 2000, and the standard deviation went down from 8 percent in 1975 to 5.8 percent in 2000.

Evidently, globalization seems to be a catalyst to a major cut in the taxes on corporate income.

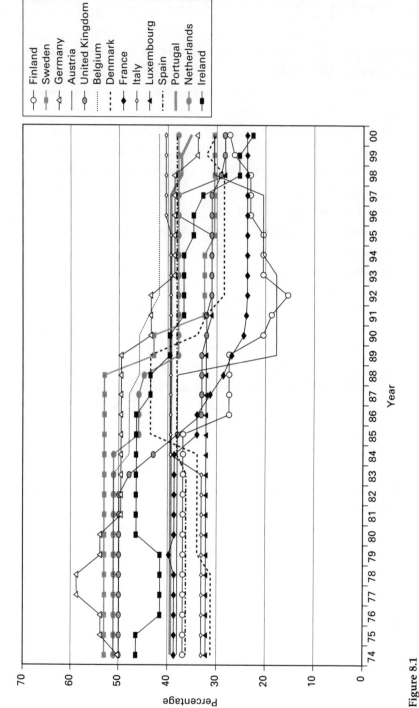

Figure 8.1
Effective tax rates on corporate income
Notes: Parameter values are $r = 4$ percent, $\pi = 4$ percent, $\delta = 20$ percent.

Table 8.1
Statutory Corporate Tax Rates in the Enlarged EU, 2003

Country	Tax Rates (%)
Austria	34
Belgium	34
Cyprus*	15
Czech Republic*	31
Denmark	30
Estonia*	0
Finland	29
France	33.3
Germany	40
Greece	35
Hungary*	18
Ireland	12.5
Italy	34
Latvia*	19
Lithuania*	15
Luxembourg	22
Malta*	35
The Netherlands	34.5
Poland*	27
Portugal	30
Slovakia*	25
Slovenia*	25
Spain	35
Sweden	28
United Kingdom	30

Note: *Denotes a new entrant.

8.4   Conclusion

We present empirical evidence on the behavior of taxes on capital income in the EU in the last three decades of the twentieth century. It points to the notion that international tax competition that follows globalization of capital markets puts strong downward pressures on the taxation of capital income.

The 2004 enlargement of the EU with 10 new countries has put a further downward pressure on capital income taxation. Table 8.1 describes the corporate tax rates in the 25 EU countries in 2004. It reveals a marked gap between the original EU-15 countries and the 10 accession countries. The latter have significantly lower rates. Estonia, for instance, has no corporate tax; the rates in Cyprus and Lithuania are 15%; and in Latvia, Poland, and Slovakia, 19%. In contrast, the rates in Belgium, France, Germany, Greece, Italy, and the Netherlands range from 33% to 40%. Indeed, Germany and France are pushing the new entrants to raise their corporate tax rates, but it is doubtful whether the EU can agree on harmonizing tax rates at a level close to the existing one in Germany and France. The latter will probably succumb to the tax competition forces and significantly cut their rates.

Capital income taxation cannot come to the rescue of the dwindling welfare states in EU-15 countries.

Notes

Chapter 1

1. These numbers are taken from Robin Brooks (2003), who reports global trends in youth and old-age dependency in greater detail. See also Attanasio and Gianluca 2000.

2. Occupational pension systems do not escape some of these implications either.

3. It is worth mentioning that the ceiling on the public deficit was in effect suspended at the November 2003 meeting of the EU ministers of finance. The ministers decided not to impose sanctions on Germany, France, and Portugal for violating this ceiling. This puts doubt on whether the debt ceiling will be enforced.

4. This calculated deficit is different from the traditional definition of a government debt, which comprises only realized liabilities (that is, liabilities backed by paper).

5. Maurice Obstfeld and Alan M. Taylor (2003) examine the historical development of globalization (in particular, international capital mobility) by political economy forces. After World War I, "newly or better-enfranchised groups such as the working classes" contributed to severely impede capital mobility. The peace and prosperity that emerged following World War II, and that intensified after the end of the cold war, unleashed political forces for freer capital mobility. See also George Borjas 1994 and Robin Brooks 2003.

6. Hans-Werner Sinn (1990) was one of the earliest economists to raise this issue. He expressed fears that the very foundation of the welfare state will disappear because of international tax competition.

7. Before Alan Greenspan became the Fed Chairman, he headed a commission that recommended changes in the U.S. social security system, to ensure its future. The most important recommendation adopted by the U.S. Congress was to increase payroll taxes. The purpose was to generate surpluses within the social security system—thus, to build up a trust fund to pay benefits once the baby boomers retire. These changes were made before the U.S. fertility rate started to rise (see also section 2.1).

In the United States, the stock marked also played a role. Many U.S. upper- and middle-class workers were mauled by the 2000 stock market decline, but the retirement prospects of far more families have been hurt by changes in the Social Security and private pension systems. In 1998, the bottom 90 percent of households accounted for just 18 percent of stock market wealth.

Gene Koretz (2002) describes a deferral of benefits in the U.S. Social Security system, aiming at reducing fiscal pressures:

Back in 1983, Congress lowered future Social Security benefits by increasing the "full retirement age" at which people would become eligible for full Social Security checks, which had been 65. However, the legislation mandated that the increase would take effect only with people born in 1938 and after—that is, folks approaching retirement today. Thus, if you were born in 1938, your full retirement age is 65 years and two months, and the age for full benefits will keep rising over the next two decades until it reaches 67 for people born in 1960 or later. This process translates into growing benefit cuts for people who choose not to defer retirement. Next year, for example, people who apply for Social Security when they turn 65 will receive 1.1% less than they would have gotten under the old formula. By 2008, such applicants will get 6.2% less, and the cuts will hit 12% when the full retirement age reaches 67. Meanwhile, those who opt to collect reduced benefits early, at age 62, will suffer a larger cut.

Chapter 2

1. Europe has been falling short of babies for 30 years. According to UN data, the average European woman of childbearing age is likely to have 1.4 children, down sharply from 2.0 in the early 1970s. The minimum needed for stable population is 2.1. The decline is mainly explained by the fact that many women have been remaining in the workforce and postponing childbearing. Japan's birth rate is falling much faster than previously expected. On governments' policies to boost fertility, see Razin and Sadka 1995a. The United States experienced a similar trend until recently, but the fertility rate has started to rise sharply.

2. This is typically the case in practice where the out-of-pocket costs of investment in human capital are not tax-deductible. In contrast, investment in physical capital is tax-deductible, albeit imperfectly, through annual depreciation allowances (rather than full dispensing).

3. Strictly speaking, the transfer is defined per family, so that the number of children in the family does not affect the attitude of the family toward the transfer. Therefore, the number of children does not affect the voting decision of the family. Also, each family (whether young or old and irrespective of the number of children) consists of the same number of eligible voters.

4. Razin and Sadka (2000) consider a similar model with variable factor returns, but the solution requires numerical simulations. See also Wildasin 1994.

5. A further distortion is caused in practice by the progression of the labor-income tax, as the opportunity cost of investment in human capital (in the form of forgone income) is typically taxed at a lower rate than the return to investment in human capital.

6. Our tax-transfer system redistributes income both within generations (from the rich to the poor) and between generations (from the young to the old). In a social security system that redistributes mainly between generations, the median (decisive) voter is naturally determined by age (see Sinn and Ubelmesser, 2001, for an application to pension reform in Germany).

7. Edith Sand (2003) shows, however, that when the economy collectively decides whether to be more open to capital flows, then the link between income inequality and redistribution is severely weakened.

8. We assume that aging occurs through a decline in fertility (that is, n falls). Alternatively, we can assume that aging occurs also because people live longer. This can be specified by letting people effectively live only a fraction of the section period and then telling their fraction to rise. If we denote this fraction by d, then db will replace b in the budget constraint (2.4); and the individual choice of human capital and saving will adjust to the shorter horizon.

9. Notice also that a lower n reduces lifetime welfare of everyone in our pay-as-you-go, tax-transfer system (for given tax rates) in an overlapping-generations framework (see Razin and Sadka, 1999). This is because a decline in n reduces the share of the (working) young in the population and their ability to finance a given transfer, thereby forcing a decline in the transfer.

10. The efficiency cost of taxation arises because taxation distorts economic decisions. In our model, the payroll tax distorts the decision on whether to acquire skills (that is, the cutoff e^*) and reduces output.

11. Because of the distortion caused by the tax, the unskilled median voter will not generally push the tax rate all the way up to 100 percent.

12. To see this, let γ approach zero. Then, as can be seen from equation (2.14), B_n approaches a positive limit of $wl\{e^*[\tau_0(n, q), q)]\}/(2 + n)^2$, if τ does not approach one. From equation (2.11) it can be verified that τ does indeed not approach one if q is sufficiently large.

13. The countries included are Denmark, Finland, France, Germany, Italy, the Netherlands, Norway, Spain, Sweden, the United Kingdom, and the United States.

14. The dependency ratio in our regressions grouped together both the elderly and children. Similarly, social transfers are all-inclusive. Recall that in our voting model it is the family that casts its vote (children do not vote). Thus, our model's predictions are consistent with the negative coefficient of the overall dependency ratio in the regressions. A follow-up study by John Bryant (2003) distinguishes between the elderly and children both in the dependency ratios and in the social expenditures.

15. Naturally, the outcome of political-economy processes are affected also by special-interest groups through lobbying activity. In the case of migration, the associations of employers may lobby for immigration, whereas labor unions may lobby against immigration; see Facchini, Razin, and Willmann (forthcoming) for estimates of these lobbying effects.

16. It could be argued that the positive coefficient of the share of medium- and high-educated immigrants may merely reflect the progression of the wage tax rather than causation between this share and the tax rate. However, the progression is controlled by the per-capita GDP growth-rate variable.

Chapter 3

1. A linear production function would attract an infinite number of migrants. See Razin and Sadka 2000 for a relaxation of the linearity assumption.

2. Note from equations (3.7') and (3.13) that positive b and τ are possible only when the wage differential at the source country (that is, w_h^*/w_ℓ^*) is lower than the wage differential at the destination country, which is $1/q$.

Chapter 4

1. Greg Mankiw (1999, p. 110) puts this argument as follows:

Having trouble saving for your retirement? Try this simple solution: Borrow some money at 7%, buy stocks that return 10%, and pocket the 3% difference. Still running short? Don't worry—just do it again.

This is, of course, ridiculous advice. Buying equities with borrowed money is a risky strategy and no one should do it without understanding those risks.

So let's consider the downside. Suppose the federal government put some of the Social Security trust fund in equities. Now suppose that the next decade turns out less like the early 1990s and more like the early 1930s, when the Dow Jones Industrial Average fell from 381 to 41—or like Japan today, where the stock market is still at less than half the level it reached a decade ago. What would happen?

Clearly, Social Security would be in big trouble. Not only would baby-boomers be starting to retire, automatically boosting government spending on retirement programs, but the market collapse would likely coincide with a recession, reducing tax revenue. With the trust fund drained by low stock prices, Social Security benefits would almost certainly be cut a lot.

Although the downside risk is far from negligible, it could still be a risk worth taking. Buying stocks rather than bonds does work out, on average, and we would be irrational to avoid risk at all costs. But there are several reasons to think it's a bad bet.

First, it seems an unlikely coincidence that the proposal (to go long on equities and short on govrnment bonds) comes on the heels of several years (the 1990s) of truly exceptional stock returns. If we take a look at history, however, the stock market isn't nearly as impressive: In the 19th century, the average premium for investing in stocks over bonds was less than 3%.

Second, the stock market's historical performance reflects a large amount of good luck. We live in the world's richest country, at the end of the most prosperous century ever; it should come as no surprise that the market has done so well. The future may give us a similarly lucky draw, but let's not count on it.

Third, some economists see the large historical equity premium as an anomaly that has already been corrected. Most measures of stock market valuation are now at historical extremes. Perhaps this is because investors, realizing stocks were undervalued in the past, have corrected the problem. If so, stocks are unlikely to keep outperforming bonds by the same margin.

Vincenzo Galasso (2002) indeed calculated the returns on her pay-as-you-go social security "investment" for the U.S. median voter in the 1964 through 1996 presidential elections. He found that they overperformed the Dow Jones Industrial Average (DJIA) in the early part of this period but underperformed the DJIA in the latter part of this period. See, however, Peter A. Diamond and John Geanakoplos (1999) for a useful analysis of the portfolio-diversification advantages from investing retirement savings in the equity market in certain circumstances.

2. The welfare state may also come under attack because of international tax competition brought about by globalization (see, for instance, Sinn, 1990; Lassen and Sorensen, 2002; and Wilson and Wildasin, forthcoming). On the other hand, Rodrik (1998) advances an opposite hypothesis that exposure to foreign trade, another facet of globalization, generates greater income uncertainties; consequently, the public demand for social insurance rises. We return to these issues in subsequent chapters.

3. The aging of the population has some bearing on individual retirement accounts too through the general-equilibrium effects on the return to capital (stemming from the induced change in the capital-labor ratio).

4. Recent models (see Cooley and Soares, 1999, and Bohn, 1999) have used an explicit game-theoretic reasoning to address the issue of the survivability of the pay-as-you-go social security system. This literature demonstrates the existence of an equilibrium in an overlapping-generations model with social security as a sequential equilibrium in an infinitely repeated voting game. The critical support mechanism is provided by trigger strategies. According to Bohn (1999, p. 206), "The failure of any cohort to adhere to the proposed equilibrium triggers a negative change in voters' expectations about future benefits that destroys social security. Since survival and collapse are discrete alternatives, trigger strategy models provide a natural definition of what is meant by social security being viable."

To support social security as a sequential equilibrium, a simple condition must be fulfilled. For the median voter, the present value of future benefits exceeds the value of social security contributions until retirement. This condition is easily satisfied in our overlapping-generations model.

5. A majority of the voters may benefit from the budget deficit combined with social security reform. The majority consists of the entire group of the old and those

skilled working young who contribute to the pay-as-you-go social security system more than the benefit (in present value) they expect to get when they retire. The minority of the voters are those who are less skilled and thereby contribute to the pay-as-you-go social security system less than the benefit they expect to get on retirement. Thus, we may envisage a two-stage voting process. In the first stage, the vote is cast on whether to allow a budget deficit to be able to implement the social security reform. The majority will vote yes. In the second stage, the vote is on the tax-benefit rates of the postreform pay-as-you-go social security system. The transition from the existing large pay-as-you-go social security system to the individual retirement accounts becomes smoother in this two-stage political-economy process.

Chapter 5

1. This chapter is based on Razin, Sadka, and Swagel 2004. Here is a recent alarm (*Financial Times*, 2003, p. 11): "Because of an emerging pension funding gap, German economic reform efforts will face a further setback. The VDR association of statutory pension funds warns that increasing contributions to the state-run pay-as-you-go pension system from 19.5 to 19.9 percent of gross wages may be unavoidable."

2. See Jacob A. Frenkel, Assaf Razin, and Efraim Sadka (1991) for a comprehensive analysis of the principles of international taxation.

3. The opposite case of $s^A/(2+n) > s^A(e)$ for all e is not possible because s^A is the average of $s^A(e)$ over all e and $s^A/(2+n) < s^A$.

Chapter 6

1. The countries included are Austria, Belgium, Finland, France, Germany, the Netherlands, Norway, Spain, Sweden, and the United Kingdom.

Chapter 7

1. If the tax is progressive, the payoff evidently would be reduced proportionally more than the forgone-income cost.

2. Because leisure time is exogenously given, it is dropped out from the utility function. Nevertheless, as before, a labor tax is still distortionary because it affects the decision to acquire skill [see equation (7.2)].

3. These rates (r and r^*) hold in essence between periods 1 and 2, and we therefore assign no time subscript (1 or 2) to these rates.

4. In a nonstochastic setup like ours, the country evidently is either a capital exporter or a capital importer.

5. Even though T may seem at first glance to be dependent on τ_D (through the discount factor R), we may nevertheless assume that these are two independent policy tools because the government can always change either T_1 and T_2 to keep T constant when it changes τ_D.

6. For notational simplicity, we assume that the net external assets are initially equal to zero, so that there is no initial external-debt-payment term in the CA.

Chapter 8

1. These countries are Austria, Belgium, Finland, France, Germany, the Netherlands, Norway, Spain, Sweden, and the United Kingdom.

2. We use the stocks rather than the flows of foreign portfolios because the former, as explanatory variables, may be less prone to endogeneity problems when the dependent variable is the tax rate.

3. As put in a survey on globalization (*The Economist*, 2001, p. 16): "Since workers tend to stay put, governments can tax them at surprisingly high rates without provoking flight."

4. For a recent refinement of Hall and Jorgenson (1967), see Roger Gordon, Laura Kalambokidis, and Joel Slemrod (2003).

5. This formula assumes equity finance of investment.

6. The present value is obtained by discounting nominal statutory depreciation allowances at the rate $r + \pi$, where π is the expected inflation rate.

References

Alesina, Alberto, and Romain Wacziarg. (1998). "Openness, Country Size, and the Government." *Journal of Public Economics* 69(3) (September): 305–321.

Attanasio, Orazio, and Gianluca Violante. (2000). "The Demographic Transition in Closed and Open Economies: A Tale of Two Regions." Working Paper 412, Inter-American Development Bank, Washington, DC.

Auerbach, Alan J. (1983). "Corporate Taxation in the United States." *Brookings Papers on Economic Activity* 2: 451–513.

Barro, Robert J., and Jong-Wha Lee. (2002). "International Data on Educational Attainment: Updates and Implications." Unpublished manuscript, Harvard University, Cambridge, MA.

Barro, Robert J., and C. Sahasakul. (1986). "Average and Marginal Tax Rates on Social Security and the Individual Income Tax." *Journal of Business* 56(4): 555–566.

Besley, Tim, Rachel Griffith, and Alexander Klemm. (2001). "Empirical Evidence on Fiscal Interdependence in OECD Countries." Mimeo, Institute for Fiscal Studies, London.

Bohn, Henning. (1999). "Will Social Security and Medicare Remain Viable as the U.S. Population Is Aging?" *Carnegie-Rochester Series on Public Policy* 50 (June): 1–53.

Bohn, Henning. (2001). "Social Security and Demographic Uncertainty: The Risk Sharing Properties of Alternative Policies." In J. Y. Campbell and M. Feldstein, eds., *Risk Aspects of Investment-Based Social Security Reform*. Chicago: University of Chicago Press.

Borjas, George. (1994). "Immigration and Welfare, 1970–1990." Working Paper 4872, National Bureau of Economic Research, Cambridge, MA.

Brooks, Robin. (2003). "Population Aging and Global Capital Flows in a Parallel Universe." *International Monetary Fund Staff Papers* 50(2): 200–221.

Brugiavini, Agar. (1999). "Social Security and Retirement in Italy." In Jonathan Gruber and David A. Wise, eds., *Social Security and Retirement around the World.* Chicago: University of Chicago Press.

Bryant, John. (2003). "Modelling the Effect of Population Ageing on Government Social Expenditures." Working Paper 03/15, New Zealand Treasury, Wellington, New Zealand.

Cogan, John F., and Olivia S. Mitchell. (2003). "Perspectives from the President's Commission on Social Security Reform." *Journal of Economic Perspectives* 17(2): 149–172.

Cooley, Thomas, and Jorge Soares. (1999). "A Positive Theory of Social Security Based on Reputation." *Journal of Political Economy* 107: 135–160.

Daveri, Francesco, and Guido Tabellini. (2000). "Unemployment, Growth, and Taxation in Industrial Countries." *Economic Policy: A European Forum* 30 (April): 47–86.

Deininger, Klaus, and Lyn Squire. (1996). "A New Dataset Measuring Income Inequality." *World Bank Economic Review* 10 (September): 565–591. Updated dataset available on http://www.worldbank.org.

Devereux, Michael P., and Rachel Griffith. (2002). "The Impact of Corporate Taxation on the Location of Capital: A Review." *Swedish Economic Policy Review*: 79–102.

Devereux, Michael P., Rachel Griffith, and Alexander Klemm. (2002). "Corporate Income Tax Reform and International Tax Competition." *Economic Policy* 35 (October): 451–488.

Diamond, Peter A., and John Geanakoplos. (1999). "Social Security Investment in Equities: I. Linear Case." Working Paper 7103, National Bureau of Economic Research, Cambridge, MA.

Diamond, Peter A., and James A. Mirrlees. (1971). "Optimal Taxation and Public Production." *American Economic Review* (March/June): 261–278.

The Economist. (1997). "Disappearing Taxes." *The Economist* (May 31): 17–23.

The Economist. (2001). "Globalization and Its Critics." *The Economist* (September 29): after p. 60.

The Economist. (2002). "Demography and the West." *The Economist* (August 24): 21–23.

Facchini, Giovanni, Assaf Razin, and Gerald Willmann. (Forthcoming). "Welfare Leakage and Immigration Policy." *CESifo Economic Studies.*

Fehr, Hans, Sabine Jokish, and Laurence Kotlikoff. (Forthcoming). "The Roles of Capital Flows, Immigration and Policy." In Robin Brooks and Assaf Razin, eds., *The*

Politics and Finance of Social Security Reforms. Cambridge: Cambridge University Press.

Financial Times. (2003). *Financial Times* (March 11), 11.

Frenkel, Jacob A., Assaf Razin, and Efraim Sadka. (1991). *International Taxation in an Integrated World.* Cambridge, MA: MIT Press.

Future Magazine, various issues.

Galasso, Vincenzo. (2002). "The U.S. Social Security: A Financial Appraisal for the Median Voter." Discussion Paper 2456, Centre for Economic Policy Research, London.

Gokhale, Jagadeesh, and Kent Smetters. (2003). *Fiscal and Generational Imbalances: New Budget Measures for New Budget Priorities.* Washington, DC: American Enterprise Institute Press.

Gordon, Roger, Laura Kalambokidis, and Joel Slemrod. (2003). "A New Summary Measure of the Effective Tax Rate on Investment." Working Paper 9535, National Bureau of Economic Research, Cambridge, MA.

Hall, Robert E., and Dale W. Jorgenseon. (1967). "Tax Policy and Investment Behavior." *American Economic Review* 57: 391–414.

Hille, Hubertus, and Thomas Straubhaar. (2001). "The Impact of EU Enlargement on Migration Movements and Economic Integration: Results of Recent Studies." In OECD (ed.), *Migration Policies and EU Enlargement: The Case of Central and Eastern Europe,* pp. 79–100. Paris: OECD.

Hines, James R. (1999). "Lessons from Behavioral Responses to International Taxation." *National Tax Journal* 52: 304–322.

Koretz, Gene. (2002). "Economic Trends." *Business Week* (August 26), 31.

Krugman, Paul. (2002). "Notes on Social Security." http://www.wws.princeton.edu/~pkrugman/.

Lane, Philip, and Gian Maria Milesi-Ferretti. (2001). "The External Wealth of Nations: Measures of Foreign Assets and Liabilities for Industrial and Developing Countries." *Journal of International Economics* 55(2): 263–294.

Lassen, David D., and Peter Birch Sorensen. (2002). "Financing the Nordic Welfare States: The Challenge of Globalization to Taxation in Nordic Countries." Report prepared for the Nordic Council of Ministers, Oslo, Norway, June 11–12.

Mankiw, Greg. (1999). "How to Screw Up Social Security." *Fortune* (March 15, 1999): 32–33.

Meltzer, Allan H., and Scott F. Richard. (1981). "A Rational Theory of the Size of Government." *Journal of Political Economy* 89(5): 914–927.

Mendoza, Enrique, Gian Maria Milesi-Ferretti, and Patrick Asea. (1997). "On the Ineffectiveness of Tax Policy in Altering Long-Run Growth: Harberger's Super-neutrality Conjecture." *Journal of Public Economics* 66 (October): 99–126.

Mendoza, Enrique, Assaf Razin, and Linda Tesar. (1994). "Effective Tax Rates in Macroeconomics: Cross-Country Estimates of Tax Rates on Factor Income and Consumption." *Journal of Monetary Economics* 34(3) (December): 297–323.

Mirrlees, James A. (1971). "An Exploration in the Theory of Optimum Income Taxation." *Review of Economic Studies* 38(114) (April): 175–208.

Obstfeld, M., and Alan M. Taylor. (2003). "Globalization and Capital Markets." In Michael D. Bordo, Alan M. Taylor, and Jeffrey G. Williamson, eds., *Globalization in Historical Perspective*. Chicago: University of Chicago Press.

Oeppen, Jim, and James W. Vaupel. (2002). "Demography: Broken Limits to Life Expectancy." *Science* 296 (May): 1029–1031.

Organization for Economic Cooperation and Development (OECD). (1991). *Taxing Profits ina Global Economy: Domestic and International Issues*. Paris: OECD.

Organization for Economic Cooperation and Development (OECD). (1998). *Human Capital and Investment: An International Comparison*. OECD: Paris.

Organization for Economic Cooperation and Development (OECD). (2003). *OECD Analytical Database*. Paris: OECD.

Persson, Torsten, and Guido Tabellini. (2003). "Political Economics and Public Finance." In Alan Auerbach and Martin Feldstein, eds., *Handbook of Public Economics*. Vol. 3. Amsterdam: North-Holland.

Razin, Assaf, and Efraim Sadka. (1995a). *Population Economics*. Cambridge, MA: MIT Press.

Razin, Assaf, and Efraim Sadka. (1995b). "Resisting Migration: Wage Rigidity and Income Distribution." *American Economic Review: Papers and Proceedings* (May): 312–316.

Razin, Assaf, and Efraim Sadka. (1999). "Migration and Pension with International Capital Mobility." *Journal of Public Economics* 74: 141–150.

Razin, Assaf, and Efraim Sadka. (2000). "Unskilled Migration: A Burden or a Boon for the Welfare State?" *Scandinavian Journal of Economics* 102: 463–479.

Razin, Assaf, Efraim Sadka, and Phillip Swagel. (2001). "Political Economics of Capital Income Taxation with Aging Population." Mimeo.

Razin, Assaf, Efraim Sadka, and Phillip Swagel. (2002a). "The Aging Population and the Size of the Welfare State." *Journal of Political Economy* 110(4) (August): 900–918.

Razin, Assaf, Efraim Sadka, and Phillip Swagel. (2002b). "Tax Burden and Migration: A Political-Economy Theory and Evidence." *Journal of Public Economics* 85(2) (August): 167–190. Earlier version with numerical results: Working Paper 6734, National Bureau of Economic Research, Cambridge, MA, September 1998.

Razin, Assaf, Efraim Sadka, and Phillip Swagel. (2002c). "The Wage Gap and Social Security: Theory and Evidence." *American Economic Review* 92(2) (May): 390–395.

Razin, Assaf, Efraim Sadka, and Phillip Swagel. (2004). "Capital Income Taxation: Aging and the Mixed Attitude of the Old." *Review of World Economics* 140(3): 310–329.

"A Retreat on Tax Havens." (2001). *New York Times* (May 26), 9.

Rodrik, Dani. (1998). "Why Do More Open Economies Have Bigger Governments?" *Journal of Political Economy* 106(5) (October): 997–1032.

Saint-Paul, Gilles. (1994). "Unemployment, Wage Rigidity and Returns to Education." *European Economy Review* 38(3/4) (April): 535–544.

Sand, Edith. (2003). "Globalization, Income Inequality and Redistribution." M.A. thesis, Tel-Aviv University, Tel-Aviv.

Sinn, Hans-Werner. (1990). "Tax Harmonization and Tax Competition in Europe." *European Economic Review* 34: 489–504.

Sinn, Hans-Werner, and Silke Ubelmesser. (2001). "When Will the Germans Get Trapped in their Pension System?" Mimeo, CESifo, Munich, Germany.

Smith, James P., and Barry Edmonston, eds. (1997). *The New American: Economic, Demographic and Fiscal Effects of Immigration.* Washington, DC: National Academy Press.

Sorensen, Peter Birch. (2002). "The Case for International Tax Coordination Reconsidered." *Economic Policy* 31: 429–472.

Tabellini, Guido. (2003). "Principles of Policy Making in the European Union: An Economic Perspective." *CESifo Economic Studies* 49(1): 75–102.

Thode, Eric. (2003). "Securing Pensions for the Next Fifty Years: Achievements of Recent Reforms in Selected Countries." *Dice Report: Journal of Institutional Comparisons* 1(1) (Spring): 3–10.

Wilson, John D., and David Wildasin. (Forthcoming). "Capital Tax Competition: Bane or Boon?" *Journal of Public Economics*.

Wildasin, David E. (1994). "Income Redistribution and Migration." *Canadian Journal of Economics* 27(3) (August): 637–656.

World Bank. Various years. *World Development Indicators.* Washington, DC: World Bank Publications.

Index